JOB WON!

500,000 HIRES AND COUNTING

WRITTEN BY
PHIL BLAIR

author·HOUSE®

What People Are Saying...

"Congratulations on writing an outstanding book. I've read a lot of these and this is one of the best. It was a bright, quick paced, and enjoyable to read. Aside from it being comprehensive, covering the breadth of what a job seeker needs to know and do, I loved the tone. I really believe that "Job Won!" is going to be the new go to book."

Jack Farnan, SVP, Human Resources, Mitchell International, Inc.

"Invaluable insights from the man who really knows what employers are looking for. Phil has devoted his career to helping others understand how to manage their career and how to get the job they want and deserve. Read this book and you are way ahead of the others who will be competing for the job that you will get."

Peter Callstrom, President & CEO, San Diego Workforce Partnership

"After many years in the Human Resource profession, I found "Job Won" to be the most practical and valuable book on the job search process I have ever read. It should be required reading for all HR professionals and career transition firms to help guide people in their search for a job or a career change."

Bernie Kulchin, Vice President, Human Resources General Dynamics (Ret), Vice President Human Resources Cubic Corporation (Ret)

"I wanted to thank you again for "Job Won!" helping me find my career path. Your enthusiasm and passion for your work has made me re-assess my career choices."

Michael Bice, CDR Michael Bice, US Navy (ret)

"Job Won!" Is a practical guide on career preparation, which gives key tips about networking, interviewing, actually getting the job and how to keep it! Written by one of the Employment Gurus of Manpower, Phil Blair, it's a self-help guide that should be on the "must read" list for every young person seeking career success.

Joanne Pastula, President & CEO, Junior Achievement of San Diego & Imperial Counties

What People Are Saying...

"Your tips and insights have inspired me to new heights! Thanks for helping me accentuate my strengths and recognize my weaknesses."

Ron Donoho, Seminar Attendee

"Job Won!" is an invaluable tool for anyone in the job market. But it's also a great instruction manual for employed professionals looking to move up or to move on to something different. It's like having a coach's playbook in your pocket when it comes to the job market. Before you begin your next job search or career change, read "Job Won!".

Randy Beck, Adjunct Professor,
Lubar School of Business, University of Wisconsin

"Job Won!" has inspired me to reevaluate my resume, job search and interviewing techniques. I am now using it as my new career Bible and I have already started to see new and improved methods, knowledge and means of getting that job!

Kevin Hass, Job Candidate

"Phil Blair has built his entire career on understanding the employment market, becoming an expert on what makes one candidate more successful than another and how to win the job. Now through "Job Won!", Phil shares his expertise with anyone searching for a job, whether for their first professional position or a mid-career change. A must-read for anyone looking to improve their job search skills and avoid the common mistake made by many applicants. If you want to win the job, "Job Won!" is your book!"

Barbara Beck, CEO, Learning Care Group

"Your seminar helped me make a huge decision in the upcoming weeks."

Mark Evans Kirkpatrick, Seminar Attendee

AuthorHouse™
1663 Liberty Drive
Bloomington, IN 47403
www.authorhouse.com
Phone: 1-800-839-8640

Published by AuthorHouse 12/10/2013

ISBN: 978-1-4817-2501-9 (sc)
ISBN: 978-1-4817-2500-2 (e)

Library of Congress Control Number: 2013904584

"Every person has unique gifts,

and those gifts give him or her the power and the opportunity

to accomplish great things, if he or she learns how

to use those gifts and channel them in the right direction"

– Zig Zigler in "Born to Win"

Table of Contents

Chapter 6: Continued

Chapter 7: Congratulations, you've got the job   141

Chapter 8: Keeping a job   157

Chapter 9: Managing your career   175

Bibliography   189

Dedication

Job Won!^{SM} is dedicated to all the men and women that had their careers upended by the circumstances of the 2008 financial collapse. None of us saw it coming and it hit like a ton of bricks. The resilience of people continues to amaze me as they pick up the pieces of their old career paths and piece together a new future for themselves. It is uncanny how often I hear from people that losing their job just may have been the best thing that ever happened to them - otherwise they never would have been motivated to seek out their current position - one that they are now passionate about.

To all of you, my complete respect.

Acknowledgements

This book is the result of years of pestering, most notably by Marlee Ehrenfeld, founder and president of MJE Marketing Services in San Diego. Marlee and her firm have handled public relations for Manpower of San Diego for more than 15 years – an eon in the PR business – and for a good chunk of this time, she has been telling me (sometimes stridently) that I should write a book about what I have learned over the years about human resources and human nature.

I thought this was a good idea, but didn't act until Marlee recruited her husband, Scott LaFee, a veteran journalist and long-time science writer at the San Diego Union-Tribune. Scott has a talent for taking extraordinarily complex topics and translating them into easy-to-understand stories. Marlee talked Scott into helping me with the book. All I needed to do was talk to Scott.

Over the course of many months, we talked a lot about the purpose of the book, its structure and, increasingly, the nitty-gritty of finding and winning a job. Our conversations helped crystallize my thinking, which Scott captured in words, aided and abetted by my own enthusiastic (if not always embraced) editorial ruminations.

Beside every successful executive is an even more successful Executive Assistant. For me, that's Colette Morel, who has worked tirelessly and with infinite patience to keep me organized and on track throughout the process of creating "Job Won!," from the earliest concept meetings with Marlee through writing with Scott to final design and publication. Patrick Pierce has been a pleasure to work with as we venture into public appearances.

Last but not least, a nod to Mel Katz, my best friend and business partner for more than 35 years. When I seriously got down to writing this book, Mel stepped up and assumed most of the day-to-day responsibilities for running Manpower San Diego. Without his hard work – and occasional motivational nudges – "Job Won!" might never have got done.

And so a heartfelt expression of thanks to all – Marlee, Scott, Colette, Patrick and Mel – for their unstinting and invaluable encouragement, advice, wisdom, talent and assistance. You made the job of creating this book vastly more rewarding, not just for me but also, I believe, for its readers.

Preface

The world is facing a new reality. We are entering (or maybe we are in it now) what some people are calling the "Human Age." Human potential will be the next major agent of economic growth. But what does this mean to you and me?

What it means to us is that we need to take stock of our strengths, weaknesses, career advantages and career disadvantages. We need to be very clear with ourselves what these four are and how to emphasize the strengths and equally important how to downplay our weaknesses. If we have a great education, how do we use that education (engineer) to be our trump card over other people for the job? If we have a weakness (DUI or criminal record), how do we sell to employers that we may well be an even better employee than the next guy? If appearance is key to our career path (sales), how do we get a face to face with the hiring influencer? And if we have no finance experience, how do we get the promotion (project manager) without this experience?

I want you to understand how companies are thinking and how they see their hiring needs changing in the ensuing years. Not just what skills they think they will be hiring, but also the personality traits that they see as essential for their workforce to support their company's goals into the future. You, as employees managing your own careers, need to know where and how you fit into the Human Age. And especially how you play it to your advantage. Understand how employers are thinking and where the economy is going, and you are way ahead of the competition.

In the past, human ingenuity, endeavor and innovation led us to a new technology or a new way of organizing the world. We called these "eras." Eras were defined first by the raw materials our ancestors bent to their will—the Stone Age, Iron Age and Bronze Age. Then the eras were characterized by the domains people conquered, usually by improving technology—the Industrial Age, the Space Age and the Information Age. Now, people much smarter than I predict it will be "human potential" that will be the catalyst for change—economically, politically and socially. In this new reality, people and their talents and skills are rising to the challenge, taking their rightful place at center stage, as the world's source of inspiration and innovation. Thus, the "Human Age."

Epic shifts are moving the world into the Human Age. At Manpower Group, the corporate headquarters for our Manpower franchises, strategic planners are adapting to a new paradigm. They are clearly ahead of the curve in their thinking. Global economic forces have strained existing systems to such a point that they are no longer sustainable. These forces are now simultaneously converging, forcing societies and political and economic systems to involuntarily adapt. Corporations all over the world are evolving their strategies and structures as they relate to how they staff their business functions, therefore driving their decisions for when, why and, most importantly, who they hire.

The inescapable pressure of international competition is forcing companies to do more with less and has awakened employers to the true power of human potential. They know that with the right people in the right places at the right time, companies can achieve all they did before, and more. But to do this, employers need to ensure that they have the right workforce models and people practices in place to attract and retain the best employees.

The demand for specific skills and behaviors is outstripping our supply and training capacity. Talent is becoming increasingly difficult to find, creating a mismatch between the talent that is available and the talent that employers are demanding. This is why the paradox of high levels of unemployment and high levels of job vacancies can coexist. Talent isn't just numbers of people. It's having people with the specific skills and behaviors that allow companies to excel in a chaotic, global environment.

To thrive and grow, companies and governments will need to engage and motivate older workers with needed skills to remain in the workforce longer, while finding a way to engage and train our youth. We need to align training and education systems with the skill sets required by employers. Individuals will be challenged to maintain a "learning mindset" to ensure they continue to develop their human potential throughout their ever-changing careers. Lifelong learning is mandatory.

As the Human Age evolves, we will see talent and human potential replace capital as the new dominant resource. Look at the chart that follows to see all the changes. I want you to know the thinking behind corporate initiatives and policies so you understand where companies are coming from when their expectations seem peculiar or unreasonable. Once you are aware of the changes coming your way you will be better equipped to apply the practices in this book to make sure you are the talent-filled individual that companies will crave. You will be in control of your destiny. And you will be the one who gets to say, *"Job Won!"*

"Phil Blair along with Mel Katz operate some of the most successful Manpower offices in our operations. This book captures the philosophy and integrity that fuel their success. This is a great book for anyone at any stage of their career written by someone who has placed hundreds of thousands of people into jobs...and careers."

**Jeff Joerres
Chairman and CEO
ManpowerGroup**

20 Epic Shifts to the Human Age

Yesterday:	Tomorrow:
Industrial/Information Ages	The Human Age
Capitalism	Talentism
Access to capital the differentiator	Access to talent the differentiator
Driven by owners and companies	Driven by skilled individuals
Workers chasing companies	Companies chasing workers
Companies dictate terms	Employees dictate terms
Workers living near (or from) place of work	Workers living (or from) anywhere
Talent glut	Talent shortage
Unemployment from over-supply	Unemployment from specific demand
Technology the enslaver	Technology the liberator
Closed borders	Open borders
Migration rare	Migration commonplace
Job for life	10 - 14 Jobs by age 38
Corporate opacity; secretiveness	Corporate transparency; openness; human approach
Organisation for Economic Co-operation and Development (OECD) countries growing and dominant	Non-OECD countries growing and dominant—BRIC-MIST, especially China, India, Africa
Work for an organization	Work with an organization
Be lean and mean	Look out, not in
Size matters	Agility matters
Hire power	Hire passion
Command and control	Flexible frameworks

Introduction

"Congratulations! You've got the job."
Mike had worked hard to hear those words.

He needed to hear those words.

Months of tireless, anxious, frantic job hunting had proved fruitless. Openings filled before he got there. Prospects and leads fizzled. The rare job offers proved to be poor matches to his abilities and expertise. The money and benefits always fell short—sometimes appallingly so—of his family's needs and lifestyle.

Then came Mike's big chance: A much-coveted position at a major company he really admired. It seemed like the perfect opportunity: a senior management position with lots of challenges in his home town. It even paid well.

Mike vigorously pursued the application process, crossing every "t," dotting every "i." He thought he nailed the final interview. The champagne was chilling in his refrigerator. He thought about what he would wear for the first day at work.

But someone else got the job.

As we talked, Mike seemed stunned and uncertain, frustrated and maybe even angry. He had been a successful, hard-charging executive, the kind you see in movies and television shows. He had an accomplished résumé, a career that was a one-success-after-another story. In Mike's mind, unemployment was something that happened to other people, to people who didn't work hard, who didn't try. Now he was standing at the back of a very long line—a disappointed man.

As I listened to him, I understood exactly what Mike had done wrong. And what he would keep doing wrong in future interviews—if he didn't get help.

I've personally met hundreds of men and women just like Mike. At Manpower, my colleagues and I see thousands of unemployed "Mikes" every year, especially in difficult economic times.

For more than 30 years, my business partner Mel Katz and I have owned and operated Manpower franchises in Southern California and New Mexico. Manpower, Inc. is an international corporation with operations in 84 countries and a basic mission: To find and deliver talented, qualified employees to companies in almost every imaginable kind of industry, from mom-and-pop print shops to multinational conglomerates. The company motto is "We find the best in everybody and put it to work."

In my long career, our company has probably hired more than half a million people—and probably *not* hired three million more. That's more than the populations of Delaware, Alaska, Wyoming, Vermont and North Dakota combined. I've met and interviewed people of every possible persuasion. Each was unique in some way; each brought his or her own personality and possibilities. Yet they all shared one thing in common: They were looking for a job or a new career.

Mike had the right stuff to get his dream job. It was a matter of using it correctly. If I had spent one hour with him, I could have shared key information about what hiring managers look for in job candidates: the essential characteristics and behaviors that are attractive and, conversely, the traits and tip-offs that prompt managers to show you the door.

Human resource managers are a special breed. We usually know minutes into an interview whether we've struck gold or need to begin concocting an exit strategy and move on to the next candidate. The process is like looking for a needle in a haystack. There are always more candidates than jobs.

Mike was looking for "a permanent job." That phrase always makes me chuckle. There's no such thing as a permanent job anymore. We are all temporaries. I've had a dozen jobs in my life. I've sold ladies ready-to-wear clothing. Mel and I have investigated running ice cream parlors, vending machines and providing tours to the spouses of executives at out-of-town conferences. I've been out of work.

No one is immune from unemployment. Things happen. Things change. If you're like almost everybody else, you've had, and will have, lots of jobs and more than one career in your working life. None of it will be guaranteed. No one gets a "job for life." We should never forget that.

Mike needed a Career Manager, someone to show him how to more effectively create and direct the elements that comprise a successful working life, how to connect myriad pieces into a smart and satisfying career, how to cultivate rewarding relationships with colleagues and co-workers, how to please a boss, and most importantly, how to add value to his company.

This Career Manager would not be me.

With my help, Mike would be his *own* Career Manager.

As we talked the day after he didn't get the big job, plenty of red flags, small and large, popped up. Mike's résumé was impressive, but didn't quite match the man or reflect his aspirations. (I even found a couple of typos, which are instant death for any job application. Either the interviewer missed them or chose not to mention them.) There were glitches in Mike's verbal style and presentation that probably undermined his interviews. Mike didn't know how to follow up or effectively network.

But he was smart and willing to learn. Even in our brief time together, I could see little lights flash in his eyes, sparks of recognition of the actions he could take to improve his employment marketability and chances of success. By the time we finished chatting, Mike was eager to leave. I wasn't offended. Mike was empowered and ready to go.

I love my job. I love what I do for a living. My work and my life blend together wonderfully. I like dealing with people. I like wrestling with multiple challenges at once. I like not knowing what each day will bring, what fresh issues or crises will arise and the thrill of finding solutions. Every happening at work is an opportunity to learn something new about your job, an issue, maybe even yourself. How you see and handle change in your life defines you. Even in a bad situation, I try to find the positive and learn something that will help me deal better with a similar experience in the future.

This isn't just a work strategy. In late October 2003, the devastating Cedar wildfire burned more than 280,000 acres in San Diego County in less than a week. Almost 3,000 structures were destroyed, including 232 homes in my community. My house was among them.

I remember standing in my neighborhood, now virtually gone. Only chimneys, flower pots, burnt-out dishwashers and murky swimming pools remained. Everything else was ash, much of it still smoldering.

My house had quite literally disappeared and, with it, decades of memories and mementoes of a life shared with my wife, Catherine, and two sons. Things would never be the same, but then I realized something: There was nothing I could do about what had happened. We were out of town when the flames swept through. Firefighters had worked valiantly. They saved more homes than were lost. What was done was done.

I went to work the next day. So did my wife, a dean at a private college prep school. Of course, the fires were the big topic of conversation around the office, though few people knew about the fate of our house. I remember a colleague lamenting about the thick ash from the fires that had drifted over his distant neighborhood. To him, it represented a messy clean-up job. To me, it represented my children's art projects, my grandfather's rocking chair and much more. I was not alone. There were scores of families going through the same thing.

I know my colleague would have been mortified if he had realized how the fires and his comment had affected me. It was an innocent remark. Even then, I was already looking forward. A new life for me and my family would now need to rise up from those ashes. Rather than dwell on the loss, I asked myself what great opportunities and adventures were now possible. Should we rebuild or move to San Diego's vibrant downtown or the coast in La Jolla or Del Mar? Could I make the future even better and more interesting than the past? I surprised my wife and flew our two sons home, one from Australia, the other from the East Coast. We circled the wagons and began planning for a new future.

That probably sounds corny and trite, but I've always felt that way and I always will. Each dawn brings opportunity, a chance to do something good, new, better. That's how I look at my job. There are mornings when I wake up, realize it's Saturday and actually feel disappointed that I can't go to work.

Of course, I don't expect everybody to feel this way. Work is called work for a reason. But if you know what you want to do, what you're good at and can discover how best to match those two things, a job can be more than a paycheck. It can be a joy.

Walk into a bookstore or go online and you can find dozens of career books that boldly claim to reveal the secrets of finding a good job and a brilliant career. A recent favorite was a book whose title was something about "What HR won't tell you about getting a job!" My response: Shouldn't it be "What HR *should* tell you about getting a job?" We're not talking about trade secrets here.

These books discuss the art of writing killer résumés, of dressing for success and talking the talk with a future boss. I've read many of them. A lot of the material is just good common sense. Some books make solid points. Others are a waste of time and money. But none cover all of the essentials that are important, or present them from a new and valuable point of view.

That's why I've written this book. That's what makes this book different. It is the view from the other side of the table. Most authors have never been human resource managers. They have not reviewed thousands of résumés or interviewed hundreds of job candidates. They cannot tell people like Mike what actually goes on in the minds of people who make hiring and firing decisions.

I can.

Success for me is about empowering every person I assist—every reader of this book—to acquire and refine the tools needed to find a job and develop a career they are passionate about. Don't read this book only because you've lost your job. Read it because you want to do more with your life, your next job and with all of the jobs that follow. I don't promise the process or the answers will always be easy or quick—lasting success rarely is—but the results will be worth it.

With apologies to Donald Trump, I want readers of this book to hear those magic words: "You're hired!"

phil•osophy 101

I'm not a religious man. I don't believe in fate or divine providence. I do believe in myself. If I don't, who else will? Who else should?

Sure, much of what happens to a person is the product of sheer chance, the result of larger, unseen, unpredictable forces colliding to create circumstances that help shape and direct our lives. To some extent, we're all subatomic particles smashing about in life's linear accelerator.

But two thoughts have always stuck with me, guided me:

First, whatever happens in life, make it work for you.

When something goes wrong, don't blame others, even if it is their fault. Your life is yours alone. You own it. Make it work for you.

Second, live life without regrets.

Pause for a moment and think about retirement. Are you smiling? Why? Because on your final work day, you don't have any regrets. You don't have to think, "I should have done something different. Why didn't I ever…? I should have tried harder to…"

I want you to be able to say that your career was great. You did what you could, everything you could. You took your best shot at living up to your capacity. I think that's key.

About half of your waking life will be spent working, so it's paramount that your work be something you can be passionate about, that you enjoy, that brings you not just financial rewards and security, but a sense of pride, accomplishment and fun. Work is never work if it is fun. The sooner you can say that with conviction, the better your life will be.

It's time to get started.

Living to work or working to live

1

> "Change your thoughts and you change your world."
> — NORMAN VINCENT PEALE

> "If nothing ever changed, there'd be no butterflies."
> — AUTHOR UNKNOWN

> "Change is inevitable, except from a vending machine."
> — ROBERT C. GALLAGHER

Change Can Be our Friend

Change is a favorite subject of philosophers, statesmen and comedians. It's easy to find quotes. Some are inspiring. Some are profound. Some are funny. All are true.

Change is an inescapable part of life, and because you're reading this book, you're probably either facing it now (by choice or not), considering your prospects for change in the future or worried about someone else who is facing uncertain change and needs this information.

Change in our working lives is a constant, now more than ever. A generation ago, it was not uncommon to do one kind of work for an entire career. Like my father, employees routinely spent their entire working lives with one company, getting the proverbial gold watch on retirement day.

But those times—and that kind of job security—are gone. Today, labor statistics indicate a college graduate with a newly minted diploma will hold several dozen jobs over a career. They are likely to have three to five different careers and many jobs within each of those careers.

One confounding factor is the aging of America. We are living and working longer. When the national Social Security program was created in the 1930s, the average life expectancy was slightly less than 62 years of age. Americans older than age 65 comprised just 7% of the population.

Now, according to the U.S. Centers for Disease Control and Prevention, the overall life expectancy is slightly more than 78 years. In the last U.S. Census, the percentage of Americans 65 years and older had almost doubled to 13%. By 2050, more than one-fifth of Americans will be 65 and older. What does this all mean to the current group of job seekers?

Most people depend upon Social Security to provide a post-career safety net. But few believe that Social Security can—or will be able to—do it alone. As a result, some workers participate in pension plans, but they are an increasingly rare commodity. Fewer than half of the companies in the United States have pension plans, requiring workers and employers to develop and rely upon other savings devices, such as 401Ks, Roth IRAs, etc. But even these efforts may not be enough. Right now there are roughly 40 million working Americans age 65 and older, according to the U.S. Census Bureau. In 2030, that number is projected to be 72 million. In 2050, it may reach 88 million.

Many of these people are working well past retirement age. They can't afford not to. Or, after retiring, they have re-entered the job market because they discovered their Social Security, savings and pension funds are inadequate to support them. Or they retired and are bored to death with golf and bridge and want to stay active. These days teens are competing with their grandparents for many jobs. Younger workers can't climb the company hierarchy because older workers can't quit to make room for them.

This is the new reality, and it's both scary and exciting. If you've just lost your job, if you've been unemployed for a while, or if you're thinking about changing jobs, these seemingly dark days can actually be moments of opportunity. There is help all around you. I'm going to point you toward numerous sources of assistance, many without cost.

I can provide lots of guidance, but it will be up to you to assemble the pieces and take action. You will have to work at it. Until you accept that new job offer you *will* have a full-time job: That job is finding the new job. It seems an obvious point, but I can't emphasize it enough. Over the years I have interviewed thousands of job candidates who have approached the job search process with something less than absolutely serious fervor.

"I don't know what I want to do."

I hate hearing that statement, and I hear it a lot. Not so much because it means my time won't be used meaningfully, but because I know the pain that it causes people, to say it and to feel that way. We are panicky when we feel rudderless, don't know what we want to do with our lives, aren't really sure what makes us happy, what energizes us, and what fulfills us. In a perfect world, none of us would ever feel this out of control of our lives. And what makes it worse is that everyone around us seems to be in control, on the right track with a destination in sight.

First of all: This is not true. Many people are drowning in "fake it until you make it." An attitude, by the way, I highly endorse. We may be lost on the inside but there is no reason to let the world know. Think about people you have met who seem listless and uninspired. Do you run to help them, get involved in the situation or do you move away from them, hoping it's not contagious. My experience is the latter. And if you follow my advice to surround yourself with exciting, involved, energized people, you will shy away from what can be called "career wanderers."

So what do we do about it? How do we not let ourselves get bogged down in this quagmire, but anticipate it and head it off? Marcy Morrison, a career counselor with whom I've done many public presentations, wrote the book *Finding Your Passion: The Easy Guide to Your Dream Career* and has a career consulting company called Careers with Wings and a website, careerswithwings. com. Marcy has done an excellent job pulling together all the advice, directions and exercises to help make sure you are on-course for a dream job. She says, "Are you looking to enhance your life by finding a career that you love, but feeling completely overwhelmed by not knowing where to begin?"

If this is you, or could be you, read Marcy's book and I need say no more on this topic.

Robert, the son of a friend, and I had met for an "informational interview." (More on that Chapter 6.) He had reaped a fortune in stock options when his company—a dot.com player—hit it big. He quit his job, cashed the options and then proceeded to spend the next several years eating through the cash, much of it lost in real estate market speculation.

Now Robert was in his late-30s. He hadn't held a real job in eight years. He hadn't even really looked for a job in eight years, mostly because it seemed like a lot of work. The money and the good times were over. He was desperate to return to the workplace. His wife was desperate too. She was now the family breadwinner and she was fed up with supporting his "lazy butt." Her words, not mine.

But to be brutally honest, Robert was going nowhere fast. From an HR perspective, I thought, "Who's going to hire this guy?" He had been out of the workforce for way too long, with no reasonable explanation. It wasn't like he had stayed home to raise young children or that he had spent time traveling the world. Rather, Robert had dabbled in the real estate market, which clearly didn't consume 100% of his time, though in hindsight, maybe should have.

It was clear that Robert had simply dropped out of the job market because he could. He had generally goofed around. That sounds great—until you need a job. He had been a high tech guy but now his skills were out of date. He was like a loaf of bread gone stale. Why would anyone buy stale bread when there were much fresher loaves on the shelf?

I also meet lots of people who aren't psychologically ready to look for a job. They're still in shock, which is understandable.

Karen, after thirty years with her company, was among its most productive executives. She managed two departments, picking up the second job when another department head retired. Under Karen's leadership, both departments continued to shine. They were lean and efficient. Karen's co-workers liked and admired her. No one had a bad word to say about her. Indeed, colleagues joked that Karen was indispensable because she did the job of two for the salary of one.

Then she was laid off. It happened one morning, seemingly out of the blue. Karen got a call to visit Human Resources. She came back 15 minutes later to say she'd been let go. The look on her face was one of profound disbelief. It was mirrored in the shocked faces of her co-workers and friends, who genuinely believed Karen was bulletproof. If she could be laid off, anybody could.

In retrospect, Karen's dismissal was not completely surprising. Her company was struggling. It had already gone through two previous rounds of layoffs and buyouts. Karen was a victim of the bottom line. Costs needed to be cut and somebody who didn't—or couldn't— really appreciate Karen's value decided her salary could be saved.

On that fateful morning, Karen took the news with quiet grace. That was her natural demeanor, but inside she was devastated. She was a middle-aged middle manager. She was talented and well-paid. Lots of people fit her description; lots of people like her are unemployed.

Karen almost immediately began making plans to find a new job, but it wasn't until weeks later that she began getting traction in her search. It wasn't for lack of physical effort. She drew up the appropriate lists. She made the calls. She pounded the pavement. The problem was mental. Karen was in a robotic trance. There was a part of her, a collection of neurons buried deep in her brain that simply couldn't accept the fact she was unemployed. It took time and reflection to grapple with that dismaying reality and, ultimately, to put it aside. She needed time to decompress, in her own way and on her own terms. It's the same—and different—for all of us.

Once Karen had done that, her job search became more energetic, enthusiastic and focused. Would-be employers noticed and Karen, happily, found a new job doing something she liked even better.

Many newly minted members of the unemployed think their job experience or their job expertise or their reputation in the business world will act as a beacon. They are convinced a new job will find them. Sitting on the couch and waiting for the phone to ring is their version of a job search. Sometimes it's a simple case of overconfidence. The realities of the current job market will soon knock that confidence down. The reality of the situation is that more often than not they've never really had to search for a job, or they haven't done a job search in a very, very long time.

Either they stayed with one employer for years and years, moving up the hierarchy, or another company or a headhunter approached them with a new opportunity and stole them away from their current job. If I am describing you right now then I'm sure glad you are reading this book. You are in good company. You'd be amazed at the number of senior executives I've met who said they hadn't updated their résumé in years, even decades. Some never even needed one. For them, creating a résumé was a bit like translating the Rosetta Stone. It was a language they did not speak.

Jake, an HR executive I met several years ago, was laid off. He was a consummate professional that knew the business of human relations and corporate personnel management inside and out, upside and down.

But, like Karen, Jake was suddenly laid-off in a company cost-cutting move. Jake was similarly befuddled, maybe more so because he had been with this particular company for his entire 22-year career. In that time, he'd never considered another employer or place of employment. Jake had seen hundreds, if not thousands, of job résumés over the years, but he hadn't put one of his own together since college. He needed to start from scratch—and he needed help. He knew it, asked for it, got it and moved on. Jake has since found a new job.

Are You Prepared?

Some people just aren't prepared to do the work required to find a job in today's economy. If I accomplish nothing else with this book, I want to get to those of you who have been laid off, are going to be laid off or are unhappy with their current job, and give you a wake-up call. It's a new world out there. It's not going to adjust to you. You are going to need to adjust to it. This is no time to relax. Finding yourself unemployed is not the time to plan a vacation or get around to doing those long-standing fix-it jobs around the house. How many people do you know who have found jobs by staying home? How many jobs come knocking at the door while you're watching HBO? The job search is a process you must own. Now is the time to rev your engines and get your competitive juices flowing. There are great jobs out there waiting for someone like you. Your goal is to make sure it's you who gets the job. When you hear about someone else getting a job that you would have wanted I want you to be politely happy for them and internally mad that it was them and not you. This is a competition and someone is going to win. I want it to be you. There are no limits to the things you can do and there is no stopping until you have reached your goals.

In 1999, Richard Bolles, the author of the very successful and enduring book *What Color is Your Parachute?: A Practical Manual for Job-Hunters and Career-Changers* was asked by a magazine writer what had changed about finding a job since he published the first edition in 1970. Bolles replied that the more important question was: What had remained constant?

"Human nature," he said. "It doesn't change and people don't like rejection, they never have and never will."

Changes in life are frequently emotional. Job change is no exception.

It can be a roller coaster of highs and lows, fraught with depression, fear, insecurity, anger and withdrawal, alternating with hope, excitement and a sense of rejuvenation and satisfaction when you finally "nail" that new job.

If you've just lost a job, don't be afraid to feel bad about it. Be prepared for negative emotions, but work hard to find closure, especially on lingering, unresolved emotional issues. Your friends and family can help, but so too can support groups. Don't be afraid to seek help. You're not alone, especially with this book in hand.

Work defines us. Go to any gathering and someone will invariably ask what you do for a living. Our jobs are typically the number one topic of conversation when new people meet. It's one of the ways people initially size us up. "What do you do for a living?" they ask. Heaven help you if you don't have a good answer. Is it so surprising that we (particularly men) invest so much of our identities in our jobs?

When the job vanishes, so too does a bit of ourselves—at least temporarily. I've known dozens of people who were utterly adrift when unemployed.

Francisco, a mechanic I once knew, was a wild and crazy storyteller. His tales were largely unbelievable, but they were amusing and Francisco told them with gusto and panache.

When the garage where he worked suddenly closed, Francisco found himself without a job for quite awhile. He was a good mechanic, so he eventually found work, but not for weeks, During that time, Francisco was a different man. I'd bump into him at the coffee shop. He'd smile wanly, but offer no story or vignette. Without regular work and paycheck, I suspect Francisco felt a little ashamed and in no position to tell tall tales.

He got through his rough patch by working hard to find a new job. His friends helped. They laughed, smiled and encouraged. They insisted Francisco's fortunes were bound to change. They were wonderfully supportive at a time when he really needed it.

Focus on the Positive

The message here is to focus on the positive. Emphasize the good and do whatever you can to promote, perpetuate and accentuate a forward-thinking, optimistic frame of mind. You may very well become one of those people who, at the end of their job search, declares that "getting fired was the best thing that ever happened to me." Without that shove out the door, they might have fossilized in the same boring job for years, maybe forever.

Instead, they discovered a new job or career they could be passionate about, that motivated and inspired them. They stepped out of their comfort zone and into an exciting new life. You don't have to be fired to be motivated to find a new job or a new career. Stop right now and think about whether you are happy in your current position. If you are, terrific! Know that you are in a minority of employed people. But perhaps things could be even better. It's always easier to find a job when you have a job. A job search when you are employed means you are the master of your fate. You are being proactive. HR folks like me love that! We love enticing an employed person to leave their current job and join our company. We are very competitive too. We enjoy the sense of victory when we hire a great new employee.

When you are looking for work after being laid off there's always that lingering cloud that you are damaged merchandise—no matter how unfair or untrue it may be. HR folks naturally wonder why your former employer let you go and not someone else? Why were you not the last one standing? Why should they take a chance? Not to fear. There are great ways to respond to these questions, ways to assuage us paranoid HR folks.

Before you head out on that first job interview, it is critical to prepare. What follows is a simple process that entails taking a series of concrete actions. Some are easy; some are not. Some are simple; some are more complicated. Some may ask only questions requiring impulsive responses with little thought, while some demand that you be introspective, thoughtful and perhaps do a bit of soul-searching.

Physical Health Matters

But first, let's start with your physical health. For any job search to be successful, you must take care of yourself. You must exercise and eat right. You have to be at your fighting weight. Maybe in your last job you could claim that you were simply too busy to pursue a healthy lifestyle. Even if that was true, it's not true now.

Physical activity and a good diet are essential. Between the two of them they provide the energy and stamina to conduct an effective, prolonged job search. They also boost your self-image. When you are at your proper weight, when your posture is straight, and when you are not winded climbing a set of stairs you will feel much better about yourself. Believe me, it will be noticed by others, especially HR, and it will definitely improve your job prospects. Another aspect of getting in shape is that it becomes an area of your life in which you can take control, you make it happen, and in a job search situation where you feel like absolutely nothing is in your control, it makes you feel really good.

If you already have a good exercise regimen, stick with it. Improve it, if you can. Adapt it to your new circumstances. That might mean jettisoning the expensive fitness club membership with its high-tech treadmills and elaborate weight machines. But you can still jog around the neighborhood and do calisthenics or join an inexpensive neighborhood YMCA.

If you don't have an exercise program, create one. Don't hesitate to ask for help in this area too. This is not the time to hurt your back and be laid up for weeks. Concentrate on sports or activities you can do while looking for a new job. When you don't have a job, it's probably not a good time to take up mountain climbing or golf. Just make sure the activity is enjoyable, and not merely another task for the day.

Staying in shape is important to me. Part of the reason, admittedly, is ego, but I also want to stay healthy for as long as I can. For a lot of people, jogging is the go-to activity. It's relatively cheap: All you need is a decent pair of shoes and you can pretty much do it anywhere.

For years, I avoided running. It seemed unduly boring, monotonous and, above all, exhausting. Then one day my workout buddies and I realized that spending all of our time working out in a basement gym meant we were missing the glorious weather and sights of San Diego. So we evolved into a running group called "The Turtles." Our motto was "Start slow, and taper off." We don't care about speed. We talk while we run. We laugh a lot. And before we know it, our 5K is finished and we're back at the gym. We even got to know our local morning show weather man who does his reports from the downtown sidewalk outside of the station. We ended up getting on TV twice a week for a morning update on our run. We became celebrities. I can't tell you how many people would stop us and say, "Aren't you the turtles from TV?"

It's not a workout if you're having fun. Keep that in mind. Make sure your exercise program is enjoyable, even something you look forward to. Dreading is not allowed.

Exercise produces obvious benefits, and surprisingly quickly. First of all, it's a great stress reducer, which is especially valuable when your stress levels are likely to be higher than normal. You'll have more energy and you'll look healthier. Suits will hang better; dresses will fit the way they're supposed to. That makes you a much more attractive job candidate. It shows that you take responsibility for your health and appearance and that you work to maximize both. Active people radiate an energy and healthfulness that employers notice almost immediately. Even if we aren't fully conscious of the reason for the glow.

"When a job applicant first walks into an interview, I immediately size them up in terms of their general appearance," one employer told me recently, echoing a sentiment I hear often.

"I look at their clothes. That's kind of automatic. But I also—and this is kind of subconscious—consider how they carry themselves. Are they standing straight? Are they smiling, with bright teeth and eyes? Do they walk well? If someone comes in slouched, if they're grossly overweight, disheveled or something just presents wrong, they are immediately at a disadvantage. They might have a brilliant résumé. They might be perfect for the job. But if they look or sound or smell unhealthy, if they're weird or somehow off-putting, I can't help but wonder: If this is how they present themselves on a day when they're trying to impress, what will they look like six months into the job?"

You now work hard at the gym for the sake of your appearance and health. Don't let me know you have any bad habits, such as inappropriate use of alcohol or that you smoke. You wouldn't show up for an interview with booze breath, so don't show up smelling of smoke. If a candidate ever smells like smoke, they are dead on arrival. Two reasons: One, they smell so bad I question their judgment just as I would if they smelled like booze and two, smoking is an addiction that I think people need to take responsibility for. Nobody can convince me it tastes good, smells good and is not bad for your health. If your judgment is flawed enough to ignore all the warning signs about smoking, then I question your judgment in lots of areas. Of course, remember I live in California. We may be a little crazy about this health thing, especially smoking. But keep in mind "I have the gold (a salary) and I make the rules." I will not tell you that you did not get the job because of offensive odor or habits but why give me the opportunity to pass you by when it is something you can control?

Mental Attitude Matters

The second part of the process is mental.

As I've said before, "Don't dwell on the negative." Aimless doubt and self-questioning never helps. Worrying rarely does anything constructive. Likewise with placing blame. Negativity just eats up your energy and it won't get you any closer to your goals.

Frank, a 39-year-old computer technician lost his job when his company down-sized. Frank had a wife and a son in elementary school. He had a mortgage and debts. He was not unlike the vast majority of us. The average American family is just three missed paychecks from homelessness.

The layoff surprised Frank. We all tend to think these things happen to other people. Frank's real problem came after he lost his job: He just couldn't let go and move forward. He appealed to his bosses, which isn't necessarily a bad move if you believe you have a compelling argument for reversing their decision.

But appealing is always a long shot and rarely succeeds. It didn't work for Frank, who simply saw that co-workers had not been laid off and wondered why him and not them. It wasn't that he wished his colleagues ill as much as it was the notion that he had been mistreated and disrespected. That wasn't true, but Frank allowed the notion to become dogma. He thought of himself as a target and scapegoat. He was angry and self-pitying. He turned himself into something of a martyr. It corrupted his thinking and crippled his efforts to get on with his life.

Last time I saw Frank, he was still looking for work.

Here are two unfortunate employee/employer situations: When an employee gives his or her notice and the current employer matches or beats the other offer and the employee stays; or when an employee is laid off and talks the employer into letting them stay. In both cases, the employer/employee relationship is tarnished and within one year, 75% of the people are gone for the original reason or another one. You just can't go back. Why you lose a job usually doesn't matter after you've lost it. It's old news. Potential employers are more concerned about your future with them than about your past with another company. Bad thoughts bring bad karma. They cause you to stall and backtrack as you unconsciously undermine yourself, your plans and your ambitions.

Family and friends can help. If you're married or in a significant relationship, a nurturing, encouraging partner can do wonders, psychologically and practically. Likewise with close friends who can serve as sounding boards and a support team.

Avoid friends and acquaintances who, well-meaning or not, dwell on the downside. You don't need or want a "pity party." Sitting around complaining or feeling sorry for yourself and your situation is self-defeating. You'll just feel worse.

Finances

Taking action is a big step toward feeling better. When you become unemployed, it's essential to assess your financial and personal situation. You're no longer receiving a paycheck. Hopefully you negotiated a reasonable severance package. Now the goal is to make it last as long as possible. That means making adjustments to your lifestyle that reflect this new, but temporary, reality.

Sit down with your spouse/partner and family accountant. Crunch the numbers. Be honest and open, both with yourself and with your family. Don't hide the facts. Don't pull that stunt from the film *The Full Monty*.

Remember the movie The Full Monty? Most people remember the last scene with the men's striptease dance. But what struck me was the middle-aged business executive who loses his job and keeps that minor detail hidden from his wife for more than a year! He is too embarrassed about being fired to tell anyone other than his fellow unemployed workers. After all, he was an executive and people respected him because of his authority. He trooped off to work each morning with his briefcase and lunch. Where he really went was the union hall to hang out all day until quitting time. Of course, whenever he was home he had a terrible attitude, was depressed and irritable.

His wife, not realizing there was no steady income any more, spent money as usual. It drove her jobless husband crazy. Eventually, their savings were consumed and the husband was forced to reveal that he had lost his job and had been unemployed for more than a year. Now, not only was he out of work but they were financially ruined and their relationship was a wreck too. All of this time he could have been looking for a new job with the support of his wife and the community.

His story was poignant and painful.

When there is a need, all of us can make significant trims to our budgets and feel better for doing it. But even if it hurts, it's important. One approach is to make the cost-cutting a challenge for everybody concerned. Make it a game. See how little you can spend at the grocery store. Ask family members to devise the tastiest, but least expensive, meal possible. Dare them to come up with the best cost-cutting idea.

Here is mine. It's a recipe for a casserole called "Full of Bologna." When Catherine and I were first married I painted dorm rooms on campus and she was a receptionist for a photographer. Rent for our house was $75.00/ month in Stillwater, Oklahoma, home to our alma mater, Oklahoma State University. We had little money but great fun making what resources we did have go as far as they could. Catherine made this recipe once. We decided once was probably enough.

 Full of Bologna (the Recipe)

One box scalloped potatoes
One can mushroom soup
One pound bologna, chopped into cubes
Mix all together and follow the directions on the box of potatoes

Serves four

phil•osophy 101   **2**

There are many times in our lives when we just don't have a clear idea about where our careers are headed, where they should be headed and, more practically, how to get there. It's a mouthful just to say. It can start in high school when we want, or need, a summer job. It can be in college when we agonize over what major to pick, feeling like it's a life sentence to that area of study. And of course it can be in the beginning, middle or even toward the end of our working life, when either we are ready for a change, or circumstances is ready to have us make a change.

Everything in the workplace seems to be changing at warp speed. Skills that were in demand are suddenly rendered irrelevant. Talents that are newly in demand take years to learn and require going back to school. Sometimes you can't even pronounce the job titles, let alone master them. Uncertainty is unsettling, even in a good job market. In a bad one, it is downright terrifying.

It can seem like everybody else knows more than we do. They appear to have a job, or a career or at least a plan. They know what they want to do. They know what makes them happy in a job. And maybe they really do, for now. But times and situations change, when we least expect them or are prepared for them to change. Believe me, everyone faces a career crisis sooner or later.

In this chapter you will learn about imagining your ideal job. No worries about pay, education, location or any other reality-changers. This is your time to dream. I make this suggestion to get people out from under their self-imposed constraints. I want "Oh, I could never do that!" converted into "How cool would that be!" Now, you may never get to the perfect job, but it would be nice to recognize it if it was in front of you. I think dreaming of the ideal job shows we are optimists. We are empowering ourselves to seek for the best for ourselves. Our cup is way past half full, it's running over.

There is a country song that goes something like, "If you don't know where you are going, you just might end up anywhere." I don't want you to just end up anywhere. It always makes me sad when I meet someone winding down a career who tells me he or she isn't sure how they got into their line of work, how they've always been bored or even hated the job, and they're now asking themselves why they didn't ever do something about it. I don't want you to ever have that conversation with yourself.

Be honest with yourself. Knowing who you are is essential to knowing what you want. Knowing what you want is necessary to figuring out how to get it. Getting it starts with the next chapter when we develop sample Career Plans.

So, let's move on to that ideal job, what it means to you and how to develop your personal Career Plan. One that you control. Let's put that Career Manager to work!

Making a career plan

2

> "When it comes to the future, there are three kinds of people: Those who let it happen, those who make it happen and those who wonder what happened."
> — JOHN M. RICHARDSON

> "I look to the future because that's where I'm going to spend the rest of my life."
> — GEORGE BURNS

If you're starting a new career (or planning to), it's probably for one or more of these reasons:

1. **You're getting ready to *start* college, or you've just *finished*.**
2. **You've been fired (for cause) or laid off (right-sizing).** Sure, you feel like you've been gut-punched. After all, it wasn't your idea, but, in a way, you may be pleased because this forces you to make a new start you didn't have the nerve to begin on your own.
3. **You're in a job or industry that's disappearing.** Technology and automation are eliminating millions of jobs. A merger may have made your job redundant or outsourcing of some operations may have moved your jobs overseas. Your skills may have become obsolete, or soon will.
4. **You are bored.** Your current job holds no meaning or gives no fulfillment. You have a pervasive sense of emptiness and discontent because work doesn't satisfy your fundamental desires or personal needs.
5. **Your job is just a paycheck.** You do your job well. You're successful at it, and you feel secure. But there is no upward advancement. You may work for a family-owned business or a young boss that is going nowhere soon. The thought of doing this job for another five, 10 or 20 years is depressing.

If any of the above describes you, then you need a Career Plan. The best thing about working on your Plan is that you begin to feel like you're taking control of your career and your future. As I mentioned earlier, one of the worst aspects of being either jobless or unhappy in your job is the sense that your life has spiraled out-of-control. Your Career Plan is the most effective way I know for you to get that control back.

You might be thinking, "That sounds nice, Phil, but I need a job, like, *yesterday*. I don't have the luxury of making a long-range plan. I've got to pay the rent next week."

I consider myself a very pragmatic person and I understand it's hard to think about the future when current circumstances are weighing you down. Issues facing you immediately can be lack of a nest egg, a car payment past due or what you feel may be a lack of skills to get any job. I understand that and we need to work within those parameters.

First, get a job, any job. You need to keep a roof over your head while you work on your future. You will find that people can put up with the hardest, most boring and lowest paying job IF they have a way out. Always remember the temporary staffing industry may help you find fast work that could lead to that permanent job you really want. While you are taking care of very shortterm needs with a job, you will find the job very tolerable if you know it is short-term and you know you have a plan to get out of that job.

Now that the world is not falling in on you, it's time to get back to your Career Plan.

Your Dream Job

I make frequent public presentations, discussing the job market and giving job search tips. Whether I am talking to one person or hundreds of people, I ask them to do this exercise: Take out a pen and a sheet of paper and write down your dream job. Forget about how much the job might pay or how much money you need to support your desired lifestyle. Family concerns aren't an issue; neither is geography. There are no constraints of any kind. In this moment, you have the freedom to imagine.

Often, when I give people these instructions, they look back at me perplexed. They don't understand. So I give them an example: My ideal job is to host the *Today* show on NBC. Yes, I know the job is filled. Matt Lauer has the gig and he does a fine job. Darn it! Still, in my mind (and mine alone) I'm convinced that if NBC hired me, Katie Couric would quit her job in a heartbeat and return to NBC as my co-host. All the other details are not important, like having to get up at 3 a.m. every morning or being casually conversant on Middle East politics or the New York art scene. This is my dream and I get to control it! This is my ideal job—at least right now. It could change tomorrow.

My experience is that after I give my example and people have a few minutes to ponder, some begin writing furiously while others wait for inspiration to pop into their heads. For the latter, nothing actually comes to mind.

The real action begins when I ask participants to shout out their ideal jobs and why. Soon, others in the room begin to take parts of what they hear and cobble together their own ideal jobs. That's perfectly acceptable; others inspire us all the time.

What's not okay is simply adopting someone else's perfect job as your own just because it sounds good. Unless you truly feel the same passion for the job for the same reasons, it's a formula for failure, not unlike the notion of arranged marriages. A job or career defined for you by external influences (i.e., your parents, friends, boss) is bound to end badly. Avoid it at all costs. This is your time to fantasize, don't let other people do it for you.

Often people respond by citing a sport they love, usually adding that they'd also like to earn millions playing it. Usually it's golf. Or they say it would be to work for a charity helping abused children. Or they want to own their own business; be their own boss.

The details really don't matter. The point of the exercise is simply to get people thinking.

Create Your Dream Job

Now I'm going to ask you to engage in another bit of fantasizing. I want you to think "outside the box," to brainstorm without boundaries.

What are your dreams? If anything—*anything*—were possible, what would you do? This isn't just a fun exercise. As children, most of us have fantasies about what we'd like our lives to look like. We fantasize about where we'll travel, whom we'll marry, what kind of house we'll live in—and what kind of work we'll do. I'll bet you had those fantasies, and they're important. They help to shape what kind of person you'll become.

But many people, whether they realize it or not, begin early in their lives and careers to chip away at their dreams. Often, it's a process driven by harsh realities, but sometimes people simply lose confidence in their ability to make dreams happen. They become prisoners of their own reduced expectations.

Generally speaking, 40% of workers like what they do for a living. They don't mind getting up in the morning and usually come home feeling great.

Another 40% of workers stay in their jobs because it pays the bills. The jobs are boring and unsatisfying. It's a paycheck and little more. Work is tolerable, but they live for five o'clock.

The last 10% simply hate what they do. Getting up in the morning to go to work is a conscionable act, a force of will. There are often feelings of resentment and conflict. The workday stretches on forever; they are bored to tears and may be under intense pressure. These negative emotions can affect both their work and personal lives. The job sucks and the weekend can't come soon enough.

To be in the top 10% of career satisfaction with people who love what they do, who don't think of work as work, isn't mere good fortune. I'm a strong believer in the adage that "you make your own luck." Good times are the consequence of hard work. And hard work begins with a realistic and complete self-assessment, an examination of your values and attitudes and a readiness to change.

What career path do you think has the most people in the bottom 10%?

Manual laborers? Data entry clerks? Security guards? You would be wrong. It is attorneys. How can that be? Fancy title, well respected, highly paid? When I talk to them about their career choice, I hear very similar issues. "I went into it because it paid really well and there was nothing else I wanted to do. But now all I do as a corporate attorney is extremely boring contract work reading pages and pages of legal documents looking for loop holes." Or, "As a litigator, I do nothing but fight with people all day long. The pressure to win on behalf of my clients is intense and even when I do win, they are mad when they get my bill."

In both cases, these attorneys feel they are making way too much money to drop out of a legal career and start over. They feel trapped and can't get out.

Values are principles, standards or qualities that are inherently held to be desirable. Values motivate and fulfill. They imbue work and life with meaning. Attitudes describe your feelings, perspectives and state of mind regarding people, places, ideas or things. Attitudes can be positive or negative. A healthy, successful person embraces the former.

- Acceptance
- Achievement
- Adaptability
- Altruism
- Ambition
- Assurance
- Audacity
- Beauty
- Benevolence
- Bliss
- Bravery
- Charm
- Cheerfulness
- Cleanliness
- Comfort
- Commitment
- Compassion
- Composure
- Confidence
- Consistency
- Courtesy
- Decisiveness
- Decorum
- Deference
- Dependability
- Determination
- Dignity
- Discipline
- Discretion
- Education
- Efficiency
- Empathy
- Energy

- Experience
- Fairness
- Family
- Ferocity
- Fitness
- Flexibility
- Friendliness
- Frugality
- Generosity
- Harmony
- Honesty
- Honor
- Hopefulness
- Humor
- Hygiene
- Imagination
- Inquisitiveness
- Intelligence
- Intensity
- Intuition
- Judiciousness
- Justice
- Kindness
- Knowledge
- Leadership
- Logic
- Loyalty
- Maturity
- Modesty
- Obedience
- Open-mindedness
- Organization
- Originality

- Perseverance
- Persistence
- Persuasiveness
- Playfulness
- Poise
- Practicality
- Pragmatism
- Professionalism
- Prudence
- Punctuality
- Reasonableness
- Recognition
- Recreation
- Refinement
- Reflection
- Resilience
- Resourcefulness
- Respect
- Sacrifice
- Self-control
- Simplicity
- Sharing
- Spunk
- Teamwork
- Thrift
- Traditionalism
- Utility
- Vitality
- Warmth
- Wisdom
- Wonder
- Youthfulness

We don't all hold the same values, or to the same degree. Below, I've listed 99 common values. Mark those that resonate with you, that you feel are vital to a good and fulfilling life. My list, culled from many sources, is far from complete. Feel free to add other values. *Go to Job-Won.com for the worksheet.*

Readiness to change is exactly that. Most people don't like change. They think it is often difficult or uncomfortable. It means swapping the known for the unknown, the familiar for the unfamiliar, the comfortable for the uncomfortable. Your readiness to change is measured by your tolerance for the unknown, the unfamiliar and the uncomfortable.

People want their job to reflect their values, to mean something—to themselves, to others and to their community. The measure of success for most people isn't merely money and prestige. If your singular ambition is simply to make as much money as possible in a job with little or no relation to your quality of life, then okay. Go be an attorney. But I can guarantee that it won't bring true or lasting satisfaction—even if your earnings and "toys" are the envy of all around you.

Fred didn't know what he wanted to do when he was in college. He was smart, however, and saw that a career in medicine or law could be both prestigious and lucrative. He chose law and for the next few years, worked hard to get through school and become a successful attorney.

Becoming a lawyer wasn't Fred's passion, but he landed a good job out of law school and was making $150,000 after just two years. After 10 years, his salary had doubled and he was a partner. And he was miserable.

Fred would complain that being a lawyer meant day after day of cut-throat competition and negativity. He was always in battle, usually with lawyers representing the other side, sometimes with his colleagues. He hated it, but what could he do?

His family (and to be honest, himself) had grown accustomed to a rather cushy lifestyle. He would complain and his wife would say, "Okay, what is it you want to do? And how do you propose to do it?"

Fred had no answer. Charging clients $350 an hour proved to be poor compensation for interminable misery, but Fred was stuck. And the unfortunate thing about Fred was that after we met several times he didn't want to do anything about it, except complain. His wife was not supportive of a life style change. In fact, he was afraid she would leave him. He was old and tired before his time and had given up. Please don't ever let yourself become a Fred.

Taking Action

Julie Jansen, the author of *I Don't Know What I Want, But I Know It's Not This: A Step-by-Step Guide to Finding Gratifying Work*, says there are different types of meaning as it relates to work. These types vary in importance, depending upon the person. Some people seek jobs rich in rewards and challenges. Others want their work to be interesting, an expression of their personal ideals and values. Some people work to make a difference in people's lives or in their community. Others because they like solving problems. Jobs can be attractive because they permit a certain lifestyle, promote a cause, or foster creativity or learning. Or simply because they pay well.

Jansen advises thinking about each of these aspects of meaning and ranking them in terms of importance. Doing so will say much about you and help refine the kind of job and career you should seek.

There are many ways to conduct a self-assessment. You can seek professional consultation and guidance. You can buy books or step-by-step guides on the subject. There are countless Web sites dedicated to self-analysis.

Or you can just sit down with some paper and a pen (or at a computer, if so inclined) and ask yourself some questions. The key is to be honest. You want the answers and results to match you, not some idealized notion of yourself.

Richard Bolles, in *What Color is Your Parachute?*, suggests asking yourself what kind of outcome you want from your work (and by extension, your time on Earth).

- Do you want to focus on contributing to human knowledge, truth or clarity?
- Are you concerned with human health, fitness and wholeness?
- Are the arts important to you, such as theater or music?
- Do you want your legacy to emphasize love and compassion, or morality and justice?
- Do you want to leave behind a legacy of laughter and entertainment?
- Do you want the Earth, the planet itself, to be better for your existence upon it?

One book that I've found useful is Dr. Victor Frankl's classic *Man's Search for Meaning*. In it, Frankl poses some simple questions, though the answers may be complicated:

- What were you doing when you last lost all track of time?
- What do people say you are very good at?
- How would you answer if a seven-year-old asked you, "What are you most proud of in your life?"
- Who is living the life you most envy?
- What job would you gladly do for free?
- How do you want to be remembered?
- What would you tell your great-grandkids is most important in your life?
- What excites you?
- What angers you?
- What can you do about both?

Mel and I started Manpower on something of a whim. We were both jobless. He was fired and I quit (a difference I lord over him constantly, but if the truth be known, I quit right before they were going to fire me) from management positions with a major chain of upscale department stores where we were buyers. The reality was we were lousy managers. We had lost interest in the business, didn't care and goofed off. Mel's father had a temp agency in Las Vegas. Standing in a swimming pool in Phoenix, where we lived at the time, pondering the vastness of our unemployed vistas, Mel and I decided this temp stuff was something we could do too. We thought if his dad could do that well, imagine what we could do! In truth neither of us had any relevant experience or even a clue. But we did have an overabundance of confidence.

Living in Phoenix, the one thing we did know was that we wanted to live in San Diego. We researched ice cream parlors, pinball machines, tour guides, and all sorts of far-flung ideas. But we kept coming back to temporary help and Manpower franchises. We spent a few days with Mel's father in Las Vegas learning how to write payroll and run a temp agency. Then we went out and partied and wound up sleeping off hangovers in his father's conference room. Mel's father shook his head in dismay, but apparently his lessons stuck.

We took over a sad and sinking branch of Manpower in San Diego and built it into a thriving enterprise. It wasn't easy but we didn't know it at the time. We loved what we did, were completely challenged, and everything was new every day. There were long hours and days and plenty of crises. Once, a big local electronics firm cancelled 40% of our business over just two weeks. A crisis indeed, but it just meant we had to double down, to work even harder. We loved it.

Answering these kinds of questions are merely prompts to get you thinking, to help you start a reflective process that will provide you with clues and cues to what you want, what to do, where to go and how to get there. More than that, they help you define and refine your life outside of work.

The goal, of course, is to find the ideal job. But what does that look like?

Let's do a little job diagramming using my fantasy of hosting the *Today* show as an example. Here are my values from the exercise on page 23.

VALUES

- Achievement
- Acknowledgement
- Ambition
- Cheerfulness
- Confidence
- Dignity
- Family
- Fitness
- Humor
- Intuition
- Knowledge
- Open-mindedness
- Pressure
- Professionalism
- Self-control
- Variety

What is it about this job that makes it so desirable to me?

1. The job is in New York City. Not my all-time favorite city, but indisputably a great metropolis and one of the most exciting, vibrant places in the world.
2. The job pays extraordinarily well. I once read a *Reuters* story that said the current host earns $16 million a year. I could live on that.
3. Every morning, the host of the *Today* show wakes up knowing he will be meeting and interviewing the most fascinating, interesting people in the world: the President of the United States, movie stars, Super Bowl-winning quarterbacks, the guy who ate 54 hot dogs (with buns) in just 10 minutes! It's hard to imagine getting bored at work.
4. Often the *Today* show crew has to travel to where the stories are, which means a certain amount of travel, some of it international.
5. I'd be on national television, in front of millions of viewers. It's a chance to make a mark, to be widely influential in a very positive way. And it's live, which means I'd have to be on top of my game every day, every minute.

So for me, these are the elements that I need to incorporate into my ideal job search:

1. I like living in a big, vibrant city.
2. I like meeting interesting people.
3. I like being challenged to have meaningful interactions with them.
4. I like traveling the world.

5. I like earning lots of money.

6. I like being kept on my toes at all times.

I am making progress towards defining career paths that will be of interest to me. I have my six points that I feel are very important to my satisfaction with a career. So what careers could most likely provide me these attributes?

Let's get pragmatic. There is almost zero chance I will ever host the *Today* show. There is little chance any of us will ever get our ideal job, one with 100% of the components we desire. But we can look for jobs that offer the maximum number of components. To see what the real world looks like, we'll have to do some research. Since this is my exercise, I would perhaps be drawn to researching jobs in the "marketing" field:

- Products that I think make the world better, make people's lives easier or help people feel better about themselves.
- Positions at a large company, preferably an international company that includes an acceptable amount of travel, some of it to foreign countries.
- I might also research jobs in "sales." The sales field is similar to marketing, but with some different features. I would look for sales jobs that include:
  - Payment on commission. I'm comfortable with a commissioned-based position since I find my pay being directly related to my production motivating, not intimidating.
  - High-end products or services. High-end buyers are more likely to become long-term customers, thus facilitating the building of long-term working relationships.
  - Face-to-face presentations, either one-on-one or in front of groups.

Since I enjoy teaching, sharing my experience and, most especially, motivating people, I might look at becoming an "author/motivational speaker." This involves having a product that I believe in (my book, video or CD), has multiple purchasers, and has sales dependent on a large part on my personal presentation of the topic. I would develop and own the product and be responsible for its success or failure.

Another possibility is "Human Resources." I could help people find the work that will support them and fulfill their lives. It involves the meaningful interactions and daily challenges that I listed as part of my ideal job.

Overriding all of these choices is the desire to control my own destiny. I find pressure motivating. I often go out of my way to put pressure on myself, to get my heart beating and my blood flowing. This energizes me and spurs me on to do a better job, whatever it is. As a result, I'd start researching entrepreneurial opportunities.

So now I've expanded my job search to include four main areas:

■ Marketing ■ Sales ■ Author/Speaker ■ Human Resources

Let me draw you a map of what we've done so far:

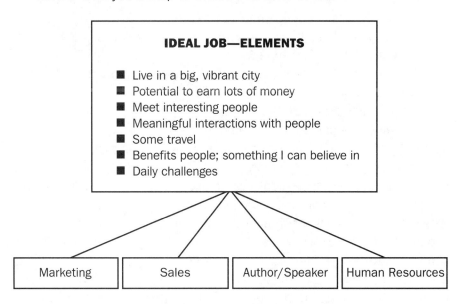

IDEAL JOB—ELEMENTS

■ Live in a big, vibrant city
■ Potential to earn lots of money
■ Meet interesting people
■ Meaningful interactions with people
■ Some travel
■ Benefits people; something I can believe in
■ Daily challenges

| Marketing | Sales | Author/Speaker | Human Resources |

Let's continue with my example, using the Human Resource path since that's where I found success.

I research job boards, advertisements, corporate websites and talk to a lot of people. The HR positions that I uncover and decide to zero in are:

■ Qualcomm: HR Supervisor
■ Hewlett-Packard: Senior Recruiter
■ Scripps Hospital Group: Employee Benefits Manager

Now the fun begins. I rewrite my résumé to highlight my education, talents, accomplishments and experiences for each of the positions listed above. When I'm done, I'll have three different résumés. Then I write my cover letter for each position to introduce my résumé. But I don't send them anywhere. If I do, my résumé and cover letter are going to wind up on some stack, or in someone's desk to die a slow death. Remember, that's an employer's least favorite way to find people.

Instead, I ask myself, who do I know who works at Qualcomm, HP or Scripps? No one? Okay, do I know anyone who knows someone who works at one of these places? A friend of a friend? You might think you don't have any contacts in the places you'd like to work, but I'm willing to bet you're wrong. My guess is, in our own communities, we are only two or three people away from just about anyone we'd like to meet. Give it some thought, go through you address book, ask your friends and relatives, use Google, Facebook or LinkedIn. Someone will come up with a name you can use.

This is the very first step in Building Your Network, a process we'll explore in detail in Chapter Six.

So I start going through the contacts in my address book and bingo! I see the name of a person whose father works at Qualcomm. I call my person and ask him some questions about working at Qualcomm. Notice I don't say I want to go to work there. It's possible I don't even qualify for the job. I'm looking for information. I call the person and ask for a personal interview. It is a powerful and important tool for you to use in your job search. When the person answers, I mention that I know a mutual acquaintance and that I'd like to ask a few questions about working at Qualcomm. People almost always say yes to such a request because: 1) there's the implied endorsement; and 2) there's no risk to them in granting such an interview. Usually, they are flattered that you're asking for their help and welcome an opportunity to share what they know.

I show up for the interview—on time, properly dressed, with my questions ready. Now when the person asks what I'm looking for, do I say, "I dunno?" Of course not. Instead, I'm very clear about the fields I'm interested in and what I'd like to do. I ask my acquaintance's dad about Qualcomm: How does he like working there? What is the company's future? I ask whatever I'd like to know. Before the interview is over, I ask him for the name of someone in HR department. In a perfect world, he will happily take me down the hall and introduce me to this person, who happens to be the Vice President of Human Resources. Should that happen, I'm on my own to sell myself as the absolute best candidate for the HR job opening.

More realistically, my contact would probably just give me the name of someone in HR. But that's okay. I call that person, using the name of the acquaintance and ask for another informational interview. I do this a few times and it won't be long before I'm talking to the person with the authority to hire me.

You remember Frank from earlier? At this stage, you have maneuvered yourself in front of some who can make the hiring decision to make or break this stage of your job search. Now you need to wow them during the interview process. This is where Frank stumbled and lost the job opportunity. Don't let this happen to you.

Here is an interesting chart from *What Color is Your Parachute?* that is a real eye opener. Start reading at the top where it says "The Way a Typical Employer Prefers to Fill a Vacancy." Their number one preference is from within, which is obvious, but they define from within to be a temporary worker or contractor. This is why temp-to-hire is so popular now. Temp-to-hire provides proof that you can do the job. You take away all my doubt as an HR person and I can hire with confidence. When you look at the typical job hunter, he or she starts at the very bottom of the cone, exactly opposite what employers prefer. How about we get you started on the top of the cone and off the bottom? Read on.

Many If Not Most Employers Hunt for Job-Hunters in the Exact Opposite Way from How Most Job-Hunters Hunt for Them

The Way a Typical Employer Prefers to Fill a Vacancy:

1 **From Within:** Promotion of a full-time employee, or promotion of a present part-time employee, or hiring a former consultant for in-house or contract work, or hiring a former "temp" full-time. Employer thoughts: "I want to hire someone whose work I have already seen." (A low-risk strategy for the employer.)

Implication for Job-Hunters: See if you can get hired at an organization you have chosen—as a temp, contractor worker, or consultant—aiming at a full-time position only later (or not at all). **6**

2 **Using Proof:** Hiring an Unknown Job-Hunter who brings proof of what he or she can do, with regards to the skills needed.

Implication for Job-Hunters: If you are a programmer, bring a program you have done—with its code; if you are a photographer; bring photos; if you are a counselor, bring a case study with you; etc. **5**

3 **Using a Best Friend or Business Colleague:** Hiring someone whose work a trusted friend of yours has seen (perhaps they worked for him or her).

Implications for Job-Hunters: Find someone who knows the person-who-has-the-power-to-hire at your target organization, who also knows your work and will introduce you two. **4**

4 **Using an Agency They Trust:** This may be a recruiter or search firm the employer has hired; or a private employment agency- both of which have checked you out, on behalf of the employer. **3**

5 **Using an Ad They Have Placed:** Online or in newspaper, etc. **2**

6 **Using a Résumé:** Even if the résumé was unsolicited (if the employer is desperate). **1**

The Way a Typical Job-Hunter Prefers to Fill a Vacancy:

—What Color is Your Parachute?

Translating your Dream Job into Reality

Now it's your turn. Use your dreams as a starting point. Dissect the elements like I did. What are the pieces that make that ideal job exciting to you? They will evolve and change, of course, but they provide some stimulus and direction for you if you don't know where to begin. For many people, that alone is a big step, an important step.

The reasons and motivations for the career you choose are limitless. They're also intensely personal. This is your life and no one but you should decide how to shape and direct it. The goal of the Career Search Plan process is to get you to ask the right questions of yourself and then apply the answers smartly. You'll notice I said *smartly*, not correctly. There is no single correct answer. There are many ways to find a good job and fulfilling career. No path you choose is irrevocable. Events and decisions you make will provoke many changes and corrections over the span of your career. And that's a good thing.

Here's something to keep in mind as you create your next dream job. The perfect job or career is as much defined by what it is not as by what it is. Think about all of the activities and things you don't like, then write them down. If you hate public speaking or making cold calls or working on commission, you shouldn't be in sales. If you hate numbers, don't become an accountant. If you can't stand to be around sick people, don't become a doctor.

The following page shows what a Career Search Plan should look like.

Now you've got a start on your Career Plan. You know more about yourself than you probably ever have before. Why? Because you sat down and "interviewed" yourself about what kind of activities makes you happy. You started thinking about how the activities you enjoy can be translated into a way to earn a living. You're on your way to a career you enjoy—not just a job that will pay the bills. You've got an idea of the actions you'll have to take to reach them. You're one giant step closer to hearing, *"You won the job!"*

I've been in this business for 35 years and this old horse can still learn new tricks. Sean, a very young cameraman at KUSI is looking to grow his career in the video/film business and I was impressed when he had business cards to hand me. When I told him to email me a résumé, he turned his card over and there it was, granted in very small print for these tired eyes. Sean had four areas of expertise with short bullets about his experience in each area. Very clever. He has since sent me his full résumé but this was enough to get the conversation going right then and there. Another version of this is putting your 20-second elevator speech on the back of your business card. Your call, but both are very clever choices.

Career Search Plan:

PROFESSIONAL OBJECTIVE: Learning and Development Professional

PREFERRED FUNCTIONS INCLUDE:
- Organizational Development
- Talent Management
- HR Process Improvement
- Training and Development
- Business Liaison
- Strategic Management

POSITIONING STATEMENT:
Learning and development professional with expertise in talent management, HR process improvement, organizational development and strategic management. My strengths include bringing structure and organization to unstructured processes, assessing talent and training needs and implementing organizational change. I am looking for an organizational development, learning and development, or talent management analyst or manager role.

COMPETENCIES: Organizational Development:	Talent Management	Process Improvement	Training and Development
• Program team assessment	• Succession planning & successor development	• Policy & procedure development	• Training program development
• Employee recognition	• Manager/Team assimilations	• Business process analysis	• Training materials development
• SWOT analyses	• Leadership programs	• Process mapping	• Needs assessments
• Coaching	• Mentoring	• Balanced scorecard	• In-house trainers

ATTRIBUTES:
- Organized, systematic and thorough
- Strong written and oral communicator
- Analytical and strategic thinker
- Customer service-oriented
- People-oriented
- Problem solver

TARGET MARKET:
Geographic: San Diego, preference for North County
Organizational Culture: Values its employees, growing, service-oriented, values learning and development's contribution to the organization's achievement of its strategic goals.

TARGET LIST: Biotech:	Health Care:	Defense:	Communications:
• Life Technologies	• CareFusion	• Northrop Grumman	• Cricket
• Illumina	• MedImpact	• L-3 Communications	• Qualcomm
• Genoptix	• AMN Healthcare	• ViaSat	• Nokia
• Gen-Probe		• Cubic	
• Sequenom		• General Atomics	
Pharmaceuticals:	**Medical Device:**	**Education:**	**Other:**
• Isis Pharmaceuticals	• Nuvasive	• Bridgepoint	• Jack in the Box
	• ResMed	• UCSD	• Cymer
		• CSU San Marcos	• Intuit
		• National University	• TaylorMade
			• Websense
			• WD-40

Career Paths: Mid-Career Correction

Many of the people I work with are in the middle of their working lives, in careers they no longer find fulfilling or they are working for a company going downhill fast. They are bored. Maybe they are all of the above. Meet David.

Years ago, David took a part-time job as a bank teller while still in college. He majored in business administration. He was a hard worker and after graduation, the bank asked him to remain full-time. He was offered extensive training and had regular job advancements and salary boosts.

David is now 55 years old and a middle manager at the bank where he started. Banking wasn't David's dream career back when he was in school. He'll candidly admit he doesn't know if he ever even thought about what kind of career he wanted. He simply followed the path of least resistance. Banking still isn't his dream job, but it's what defines him now. He doesn't know any other kind of work.

In 2009, during the Great Recession and economic meltdown, a lot of banks shrunk, failed and merged. That resulted in an over abundance of branches and a redundancy of jobs. Neither boded well for David. Through no fault of his own, David found himself laid off and out of work.

Worse, David was not alone. Twenty of his colleagues, managers at other branches in the community, were let go at the same time. David confronted a tough and shrinking job market for his specific skills with 20 other peers, all pretty much boasting the same talents and experience. And those were just people laid off from his bank. Competing banks had done much the same thing. The ranks of the newly unemployed were flooded with bank branch managers just like David, competing for zero bank openings.

David had a couple of obvious choices. He could go home, curl up in a ball and whine about the gross unfairness of it all. Or he could step back, assess the situation and get back in the game. I knew David from past community involvement projects. I considered him a good friend. Unfortunately, David was one of those people who answered my question, "What do you want to do?" with "I don't know."

Because he was a friend, I didn't suggest he come back later when he had figured out what he wanted to do. Instead, I cleared my next appointment, took a deep breath and we dug in.

We talked about what David liked and what, if he let himself dream, would be his ideal job. What did he see himself doing if he could do anything, which interestingly enough, was exactly his situation. After much discussion his four career paths emerged:

- Anything in sports
- Chief financial officer (CFO) of a small- to middle-sized company
- Leader of a non-profit group
- Founder of a new business

David had his career yanked out from under him. He hadn't planned on re-inventing himself at age 55.

When I asked David how he would distinguish himself from the other unemployed bank branch managers, he stared back blankly. He couldn't answer me. Many of these other branch managers were, in fact, friends of David's. If he sought work similar to his old job, he would be directly competing against some of his best friends and that would be difficult.

But here is the real issue: Let's say he did get the job offer to be a bank branch manager again. It would pretty much mirror his old position. "Would you be more than just relieved?" I asked him. "Would you be genuinely excited? Would bells ring, fireworks explode?"

After pondering the question for a moment, David shook his head. No bells, no fireworks. It would be a job, just a job. In that moment, David realized something: He was sick and tired of banking. It bored him. It was the "same old, same old." And it had been that way for years. David had stayed in the job and career because it was easy. He had taken the promotions and better pay and convinced himself that this was the way it should be.

But if, by chance, a suitable bank branch manager job opened up in David's community, and if David wanted to stay in banking, the person who got the job would be the person who had clearly risen above the competition, who had set himself or herself apart. Would that person be David?

David didn't know. He said that with a few tweaks and nuances, many of his peers were just as good at doing the job as he was. That's not what I wanted to hear. That's not what an HR person or employer wants to know. I want you to tell me why you are the best person for the job, not tell me you are as good as many other people for the job. If I hear that, I figure there are others out there better suited for the job. Think about what you are doing for a living right now. What distinguishes you from all the other people doing your job? If you can't tell me what makes you indispensable, then your path may be very similar to David's. If you are currently working, then start right now thinking about how you are going to set yourself apart and above anyone else competing with you for your job. And then make it happen.

Few jobs constitute one's life mission, but they should be something you can enjoy and be passionate about. Helping people find that passion is part of what makes my job so fulfilling.

Once David realized he didn't ever want to go back into banking, his next step was to begin investigating new career paths. This is a take-home assignment, but not necessarily one that requires you to sit down at a desk or computer screen. You can and should explore all your options, anything that pops into your mind during any waking moment. In fact, let your dreams do some exploring for you too. The subconscious is a wonderful thing.

Allow your mind to use free association. Let your subconscious do some of the heavy lifting. This might mean noodling ideas while showering, mowing the lawn, doing the dishes. I like to tackle tough subjects while walking the dog, when I'm free of most distractions.

In my conversation with David, we talked about his ideal job. It turned out to be professional baseball umpiring. (And I thought hosting the *Today* show was ambitious!) We soon both realized such a goal was impractical. David was too old. It takes years of working the minor leagues before one even gets a sniff of "the show." And, David wasn't really keen on the travel aspects of the job.

What aspects of umpiring did David find attractive? Could they be found in other jobs?

More digging and dissecting revealed that David was a big Chargers and Padres fan. Almost anything in those organizations seemed attractive. He jettisoned the CFO idea after concluding it might be too much like banking. Non-profit work was interesting, particularly since David's existing savings and retirement and pension plans meant he didn't need to find a job with major benefits. He turned out to be lukewarm about starting a business. He was afraid about putting his capital at risk. He couldn't think of a specific kind of business that aroused his passions. And he liked working with lots of people, not necessarily owning a small business.

One obvious career path seemed to emerge: David should pursue something with a sports team. Since he lived in San Diego, the Chargers or Padres were where he should start. He had contacts with both teams. A few calls, however, persuaded David that this was a dead-end. Neither organization had any current open positions that were attractive to him. He realized that while he loved the teams, both of them were corporations—and all that that implied. Most team employees worked behind the scenes doing jobs not unlike what David did in banking. His boyhood notions of umpiring or becoming a player in the sports business were just that, boyhood notions.

Maybe if he had approached working in the sports industry 30 years ago, David might have successfully pursued sports, but not at this stage in his career and his life. We all need to dream, but we need to be pragmatic too.

Still, David kept his career radar turned on full blast. When the president of the San Diego United Way called to get David's advice on resigning to run for mayor of San Diego, David realized their conversation might be talking about two careers changes.

San Diego's future mayor did resign as president of the local United Way, ran for mayor and won. David, meanwhile, revamped his résumé, customizing it to highlight why he would make an excellent successor CEO of the local United Way chapter. He noted his extensive financial management experience and public involvement. All of those years as a bank manager had given David a fantastic list of personal and business contacts, an invaluable resource for an enterprise like the United Way. David got the job! He paid me back by convincing me to serve as his first chairman of the board. No good deed goes unpunished.

David followed four basic steps; you can too:

1. Identify two to four potential career paths.
2. Identify companies or organizations that hire people with the skills you have in these career paths.
3. Find out if these companies or organizations have relevant job openings.
4. Learn who to contact for an informational interview.

For David, the thinking went sort of like this: okay, I wanted to be a baseball umpire, but that's not going to happen. So now, I'm looking for an opportunity to use my financial and management experience to lead a non-profit group in San Diego. I've got deep community contacts. The three organizations that I'm interested in are the United Way, the Urban League and The MAAC Project (an effort to bring self-sufficiency to low- and moderate-income families). The CEO is quitting to run for mayor of San Diego, creating an opportunity at the United Way. I can do this job. Now I need to convince the committee that I can do it.

David did, and he's now doing a great job in a position he really is passionate about.

I tell all of my clients to write their career paths in pencil. It's symbolic, of course, intended merely to emphasize that all careers are in constant flux. Almost anything can alter one's plans, from big, external forces like economic demographics to a single meeting attended or article read in a magazine.

I've had countless conversations in which a client, after spending years in a career, has plaintively exclaimed, "What was I thinking?" Their job and career has turned out nothing like they imagined it would be, and they're at a loss to explain why they've kept at it for so long. Plot a course, pursue it, but don't hesitate to change if a new and better opportunity comes along.

❖ Fastest-Growing Industries, 2012-2017

1.	Social-networking sites
2.	Street-traffic providers
3.	Green construction
4.	Social-network gaming
5.	Relaxation drinks
6.	Medical-device recycling
7.	Green building materials
8.	Retinal-imaging machines
9.	Internet publishing and broadcasting
10.	Secure data storage
11.	Artificial turf installation
12.	Online fashion-sample sales
13.	Satellite imaging
14.	Wire and cable manufacturing
15.	Fitness-DVD production
16.	Corporate wellness services
17.	Digital forensics
18.	Online office-furniture sales
19.	Online household-furniture sales
20.	Sleep-disorder clinics

Source: IBISWorld; U.S. National Center for Education Statistics; NWLC. TIME, July 23, 2012

phil•osophy 101

3

In college, I had no clue what kind of job I wanted, let alone career. After much uninformed waffling, I chose to pursue degrees in business and marketing.

My mother had long wanted me to become an orthodontist. After my parents spent considerable sums of money getting my brother's and my teeth straightened, she figured it was a lucrative career with endless clientele and no downside (apart from days spent with children crying about sore teeth).

My mom's preferred second choice was accounting. Everybody needs an accountant, she said. Including orthodontists.

For a while, I went along. Orthodontics was clearly out. Science is a language I do not speak. But I did take an Accounting 101 class and at first, everything went well. I learned that debit (income) was good and credit (expense) was bad. Then I learned debit could also be bad and credit good. The world of finance became increasingly confusing. Eventually, I ran screaming from my perceived future in accounting.

I discovered Sociology as an elective. Later, it became my college minor. I held no illusions that I would be the next great sociologist. But I always liked people and was fascinated and beguiled by the myriad possibilities of human behavior. People do strange, wonderful, and unexpected things. Their lives take turns and twists they cannot imagine. They behave as individuals and as a collective, a lemming effect that I have always found fascinating. Can mob mentality sometimes be a good thing and other times not? Who gets to judge which time is which?

Now, when I look back, I realize this fascination with people and why they do what they do marked the beginning of my career as a human resources professional.

Throughout this book I talk about always having your radar up and running at all times. This starts at an early age with career awareness programs as early as elementary school. How many times do adults ask children what they want to do when they grow up? This only escalates as you grow older and enter college. How many times did fathers of girls I was dating asked me what my favorite subjects were in school? I think they were really asking about my career focus, even at that early age, just in case I became a serious contender for her hand.

I think the main purpose of electives in high schools and colleges is not easy credits, as we thought as students. Rather, they represent an opportunity to experiment with subjects we thought might be interesting, but never knew anything about. The grown-up versions of electives are community college classes, college extension courses, even volunteer work. How many of us took an elective and fell in love with the topic. Then ended up majoring in the subject and never looked back? An interesting twist in our lives.

Finding a career path that you can be passionate about may sound a little idealistic, especially when you are anxious to find any job. I understand that. I also want you to be able to recognize a career path that you could become passionate about when you see it, at any age. For many of us, that starts with picking a college major. Finding one or more career path during your working life that you can really enjoy is the goal here.

The college plan

"Destiny is not a matter of chance. It is a matter of choice:
it is not to be waited for, it is a thing to be achieved."
— WILLIAM JENNINGS BRYAN

"If you have to support yourself, you had bloody well better find
some way that is going to be interesting."
— KATHERINE HEPBURN

"Let the world know you as you are, not as you think you should be,
because sooner or later, if you are posing, you will forget the pose,
and then where are you?"
— FANNY BRICE

The College Plan

College is critical. Higher education always pays.

Need proof? The College Board released a 2010 study that documents the advantages of a bachelor's degree in the most undeniable and persuasive of terms: relative earnings.

In 2008, the median earnings for a male between the ages of 25 and 34 with a bachelor's degree or higher was 74% higher than for males of the same age with just a high school diploma. For females, the differential was even greater: 79%.

Of course, going to college doesn't necessarily prepare you for a career. Most educated adults work in jobs that have little or nothing to do with what they studied in college. And often, writes Nicholas Lore, author of *Now What? The Young Person's Guide to Choosing the Perfect Career* with Anthony Spadafore, the folks who are doing what they learned to do in college actually hate it.

A good college education teaches and trains students to think critically and logically. It provides a breadth of knowledge and understanding about the world, and the skills to acquire more. However, from the employer's point of view, a degree is often viewed simply as evidence that the job applicant has some basic tools and can start a project—their coursework to get a degree—and finish it. It's evidence that he or she possesses determination and persistence.

Of course, after that first job, your college degree holds less sway. You'll be judged more on what you've done in the real work world. And unless you've attended a trade school, a degree does not give you the guaranteed tools to make a career.

Carly Fiorina was the first female chief executive officer of a major American company, Hewlett-Packard, and a one-time California senatorial candidate. Her college major was in Medieval Art. When she ultimately discovered there wasn't much of a job market for people with degrees in imagery from the Dark Age, she decided to go to law school.

One semester of law school was enough to convince Fiorina that she didn't want to be a lawyer. (Too bad Fred didn't experience a similar revelation.) Fiorina dropped out and became a receptionist at HP to support herself. She was a temp, but unfortunately, not from Manpower.

Fiorina proved a very good receptionist and got promoted. That inspired her to go back to school and get her Master's degree in business administration. She soon returned to HP, this time as a full-time staffer. She began climbing the corporate ladder, and the rest is history.

Every college student must choose a major. In choosing smartly, a student employs many of the same processes that are later used to find the right job and career. He or she must match their interests, abilities, aptitudes and goals to the reality of workplace possibilities and potentials. And talk with teachers, counselors, friends and family. This may be the first experience at "networking." (More on that in Chapter 4.)

Most of all, college students must look hard within themselves. And think. Imagine. Dream.

Whatever major is chosen, it is not written in stone and unchangeable.

In truth, very few college graduates have even the faintest idea of what will make them happy for a lifetime. How can they? They're just beginning the serious part of their adult lives. As Ray Bradbury said, "You've got to jump off cliffs all the time and build your wings on the way down." That's a scary thought, maybe even outrageous when one recalls how much a college education costs these days, but it's also inspiring and exciting.

So What's Your Major?

One of my pet peeves when talking with college students is when I ask them why they picked their major, especially if it's something unusual or esoteric like Comparative Religion, 18th Century English Folklore or in Carly Fiorina's case, Medieval Art.

These are all interesting subjects, to be sure, but my question is this: When you picked that major, how did you envision translating it into a real job and career?

All too often, students look at me blankly and reply: "Gee, I never really thought about it."

Choosing your major areas of study and ultimate degree requires the same kind of analysis and hard thinking as picking a career path. The processes are pretty much identical. What you study should, in most cases, be laying the foundation for what you think your first job will be. Opportunity may take you down another road. But until and unless that happens, you need to chart your own course.

My wife was also a college counselor at a prep school in La Jolla, California, where she worked. We often had discussions about the value of a liberal arts education. She was staunchly supportive, believing that one should have a broad education, find something you're passionate about and then pursue it whole-heartedly. Do that, and life works out for the best.

I like to think I'm more pragmatic. For me, college is a vehicle to prepare yourself for a vocation that will support you in the style to which you want to become accustomed for the rest of your life.

If you want to be an artist, feel free to study Italian Renaissance Art. If you want to become a minister, study religion. If you want to be a history teacher, study history. But don't apply for an accounting job with me and tell me you that your degree in philosophy makes you a reasoned thinker.

Once upon a time, businesses happily hired newly minted graduates with degrees in philosophy or history and then took the time to teach them how to sell widgets. No more. The days of IBM's two-year executive training programs are gone. Companies need new hires that are capable of hitting the ground running, who can become productive new employees as quickly as possible. From the corporate point of view, an employee is a profit center, not an expense center.

Life's too short to waste it unnecessarily on jobs we hate. As twisted as it may sound, unemployment marks a chance to make fundamental changes in our life, to make it more meaningful. College is a time to explore electives to find the initial career path that will make us happy. We need to remind ourselves to be open to several different career paths in our working lives.

I'll leave it to philosophers and next-door neighbors to wax eloquent on the meaning of life. Or what "the meaning of life" actually means. Talk to people—family, friends, co-workers, and strangers—about what makes their lives meaningful. We all can and must learn from each other.

Career Paths: College

As you work through this book and various exercises, a lot of ideas are likely to emerge about what you want to do for a living and what you might want to do for a living.

That's a very good thing. Don't limit yourself. Your horizon should be vast. On the other hand, it should begin reasonably. It makes no sense to declare that you want to do 25 different jobs—all at once. Where would you begin?

Instead, let's start with three or four "career paths" that pique your interest. It's not important whether you understand the details or requirements of these paths yet. That will come later. Right now, they simply have to feel right, as in "I think I'd really like that career if I knew more about it."

Let's consider the story of Mary, who has just finished her sophomore year at college. She is now preparing to declare a major for her last two years at her university. We met for an informational interview. Because she's still in college and quite young, our conversation began very generally. I asked about her notions of an ideal job. Mary struggled to answer. She'd never really given it much thought, at least not in any coherent, useful way. Finally, she declared she wanted to be "the new Dr. Freud and discover the cure to addiction!"

Wow. That sounded impressive, but what did Mary actually mean? Aspiring to become the next Sigmund Freud (yes, that Sigmund Freud, the Austrian neurologist who founded the psychoanalytic school of psychiatry) was unabashedly ambitious. Did Mary really want to tackle curing addiction, all addictions? It was a noble goal. I asked her to explain.

Mary's father was a physician, and she had always been impressed with his desire and ability to help people. More specifically, her father had told her numerous stories of patients he had treated for physical ailments, but whose real problem was an underlying addiction to drugs or alcohol. The addiction was not just ruining their health, but their chances at a decent, happy life and career.

As we talked, I learned more about Mary: She was engaging and well-spoken. Talking to strangers didn't make her uncomfortable, in fact she enjoyed it. Indeed, she said she liked working with the public and a wide variety of personalities. She was not daunted by new situations or sudden challenges. A few years earlier, Mary said by way of illustration, she had been a lifeguard at a local public pool and helped save a child from drowning by using her training in first aid and resuscitation. It was one of her finest moments and memories.

Personal relationships and family were important. She enjoyed working in teams and sharing common goals with others. She favored the nobility of working for a non-profit enterprise, though obviously wanted to make a good living. She wanted to stay in her hometown if possible.

After a while, step one was accomplished and, based on our discussion, Mary crafted her first four possible career paths:

1. *Nursing*
2. *School teacher*
3. *Drug and/or alcohol addiction counselor*
4. *Human Resources professional*

Mary was thrilled. These were very different career trajectories, but Mary could see commonalities among them. Each presented different, yet exciting, opportunities.

Step two for Mary was to begin learning as much as she could about each of these career paths, from the academic requirements to the nitty-gritty of actually doing the job. Mary was able to do much of this research herself by visiting libraries, surfing the web online, contacting professional groups and, most of all, talking to people in those fields.

All four of Mary's possible career paths shared traits and features. Mary was eventually going to have to focus on the path she found most attractive and practical. Yes, that does have to be considered. Before she ever went on her first real informational interview to learn about her career choices, she would need to answer a first key question: What kinds of companies or organizations in her hometown hire people in these career paths?

The answer was hospitals and doctor's offices for nursing, public and private schools for teaching, rehabilitation clinics and the like for addiction counseling and any interesting company with an employee relations office for HR.

Now the harder part, step three: Who does Mary know who works in a hospital, a school, a rehab clinic or in HR? Maybe no one. Does Mary know anyone who knows someone else who does? A friend of a friend? Mary's next big step is to get in front of someone currently working in one or more of these areas and ask them lots of questions: How did they get to where they are? What do they like or dislike about their job or career? What would they do differently?

The last question is bound to provoke discussion. No job is perfect; no career unencumbered by speed bumps and detours. Almost everybody has cautionary advice to give. Along with the laudatory stuff, it's important to hear these negatives. You want to see and know the whole picture. You don't want any big, bad surprises later if you can avoid them.

For example, Mary had very idealistic notions about teaching. What could be more wonderful than working with children? But in her eventual discussions with living, breathing, very hard-working teachers, she discovered there are plenty of daily difficulties and aggravations: chronic budget shortages (many teachers spent good chunks of their own paychecks buying ordinary classroom supplies), meddling administrators, parents who were chronically upset, or worse, indifferent.

Mary's Career Plan:

NURSING:	SCHOOL TEACHER:	COUNSELOR:	HRPROFESSIONAL:
Sharp: John	San Diego Unified	McDonald House	Qualcomm
Scripps: Devin		Mental Health System	Sempra
Kaiser: Aunt Jane		County of San Diego	Manpower
			ARC

CONDUCT INFORMATIONAL INTERVIEWS:

Mental Health Systems
Dr. Jones – Scripps
Ms. Smith – College Counselor

JOB OPENINGS:

Scripps – Emergency Room
Sharp – Pediatrics
Chicano Clinic – Internal Medicine

MAKE YOUR SELECTION:

School Counselor

CAREER CORRECTION:

Drug and Alcohol Counselor

For most of the teachers Mary spoke with, these negatives weren't enough to drive them from the field. They generally loved their jobs, though some candidly admitted that if they had known back then what they knew now, they might not have joined the teaching fray. Because Mary had done her homework, she was a step ahead. Teaching was a great profession, Mary thought, but it was not for her. The negatives outweighed the positives.

So she checked off one potential career path and moved on, repeating the process of investigation and interview as she pursued other possibilities. It took time. It takes time. But it is time well spent. This is your life. Do it right.

One other thing about Mary and her search: As you go through this process of finding and defining a career path, keep your mind and options open. Mary began with specific paths. During her inquiries, she discovered school counseling, which seemed to combine many of the attractions of all four paths in one job. She could work with kids, some troubled by drugs or alcohol. She could be an educator and public speaker. She could counsel parents and students about opportunities and goals. She could stay in her hometown. Being a school counselor appeared to be the best of all worlds, and while the job had its negatives, they paled in comparison to the rewards.

Step four: The obvious one, finding a school-counseling job.

Mary went from thinking about something in the healthcare profession like her physician-father to school teacher to school counselor. But that's not the end of her story. She didn't stay a school counselor for long.

Step five: A series of big and small events involving her students with drug issues ultimately led Mary to a career at a drug and alcohol rehabilitation center, which was one of her original career paths. She couldn't be happier. She's helping people, literally changing their lives. She's teaching them how to make good decisions and take control.

Mary is managing her career and chosen profession. I emphasize chosen because Mary did exactly that: She researched her options and chose something that was right for her. She didn't fall or drift into her job. She picked it. A lot of people can't say as much. Now, she's working on a Master's degree in counseling. She might not ever find a cure for addiction, but Dr. Freud would say she's very happy nonetheless.

Never underestimate the power and influence of summer jobs, internships, and job shadowing experiences. Think how much more knowledgeable Mary would be about her potential school major choices and later career choices if she had worked in the field during the summer, had an internship during school, and had job shadowed people successfully working in and of the job fields she was considering. And it doesn't stop there. When you are applying for a job, especially your first one out of school, employers are going to want to know what you did with your free time. Did you lifeguard, work on your tan, or perfect your golf game? Not a good sign of a hard driving new employee. Instead, if you worked in the field, did volunteer work, or took extra classes, you will be way ahead of the competition for that job. Or any job for that matter.

I would never suggest you select a college major, career or job solely on what it pays, but I do believe in having your eyes wide open to the realities of what different vocations pay. Here are the top-paying college degrees and the worst paying. You will clearly see trends in different college departments.

The Top-Paying College Degrees (2010)

	COLLEGE DEGREE	STARTING MEDIAN PAY	MID-CAREER PAY
1.	Petroleum engineering	$93,000	$157,000
2.	Aerospace engineering	$59,400	$108,000
3.	Chemical engineering	$64,800	$108,000
4.	Electrical engineering	$60,800	$104,000
5.	Nuclear engineering	$63,900	$104,000
6.	Applied mathematics	$56,400	$101,000
7.	Biomedical engineering	$54,800	$101,000
8.	Physics	$50,700	$99,600
9.	Computer engineering	$61,200	$87,700
10.	Economics	$48,800	$97,800
11.	Computer science	$56,200	$97,700
12.	Civil engineering	$53,500	$93,400
13.	Statistics	$50,000	$93,400
14.	Finance	$47,500	$91,500
15.	Software engineering	$56,700	$91,300
16.	Management info. systems	$50,900	$90,300
17.	Mathematics	$46,400	$88,300
18.	Government	$41,500	$88,300
19.	Information systems	$49,300	$87,100
20.	Construction management	$50,400	$87,000

The Worst-Paying College Degrees (2010)

	COLLEGE DEGREE	STARTING MEDIAN PAY	MID-CAREER PAY
1.	Child and family studies	$29,500	$38,400
2.	Elementary education	$31,600	$44,400
3.	Social work	$31,800	$44,900
4.	Athletic training	$32,800	$45,700
5.	Culinary arts	$35,900	$50,600
6.	Horticulture	$35,000	$50,800
7.	Paralegal studies/law	$35,100	$51,300
8.	Theology	$34,700	$51,300
9.	Recreation & leisure	$33,300	$53,200
10.	Special education	$36,000	$53,800
11.	Dietetics	$40,400	$54,200
12.	Religious studies	$34,700	$54,400
13.	Art	$33,500	$54,800
14.	Education	$35,100	$54,900
15.	Interdisciplinary studies	$35,600	$55,700
16.	Interior design	$34,400	$56,600
17.	Nutrition	$42,200	$56,700
18.	Graphic design	$35,400	$56,800
19.	Music	$36,700	$57,000
20.	Art history	$39,400	$57,100

Source: Payscale, Inc.

There are lots of lists of everything and you can probably find one to say what you want it to say. However, I found this list of hot careers very interesting:

 ## Hot Careers for College Graduates (2011)

A recent study conducted by the University of California, San Diego Extension, looked at the "hottest" jobs for college grads, recent and mid-career. These aren't the sexiest or most glamorous occupations (sorry, the world's apparently got enough rock stars), but they're what the world needs now. And they pay.

1. **Health care case management.** These are the people who serve as health care advocates for patients, helping them understand and negotiate treatments and coverage.

2. **Financial examination and internal auditing.** With companies collapsing, merging, expanding, etc., accountants are needed in great numbers. The Bureau of Labor Statistics predicts 41% growth in the field.

3. **Mobile media.** There are 4 billion cell phones in the world. Half the population has one; the other half seems likely to get theirs sooner rather than later. That means a huge demand for folks to invent and develop new services and applications.

4. **Health care information technology.** As medicine becomes ever-more advanced, so too do the technologies required to maintain enormous databases of patient information.

5. **Data mining.** Virtually every bit of the world is being converted into a byte. All of that information must be culled, sorted, rearranged and examined by people who know how to sift through a digital haystack for invisible trends and needles of knowledge.

6. **Geriatric health care.** The country is getting older.

7. **Occupational health and safety.** Technological advances, new and changing regulations and increased public expectations have resulted in a greater emphasis upon "safety."

8. **Spanish/English translation and interpretation.**

9. **Sustainable business practices.** Some people say that by mid-21st century, most, if not all, jobs will be green.

Emerging Employers

Employment is like evolution: Things change over time. A full-time, lifetime position in manufacturing used to be a norm, now it's an endangered species verging on extinction.

In his 2011 State of the Union address, President Obama talked about "winning the future." For job seekers, that starts with winning a job. And that often starts with figuring out what kinds of jobs will be available in the future and what kind of training or education you'll need to win one of them.

In a book called *Closing America's Job Gap: How to Grow Companies and Land Good Jobs in the Age of Innovation,* authors Mary Walshok, Tapan Munroe and Henry DeVries highlight the 10 most innovative sectors where they predict jobs will be most abundant. Some are obvious, some less so. Anything here pique your interest? Or get you thinking about another area of interest?

Embedded engineering. These are the people who design the software and processors that make things like iPods and cell phones do the things we have come to expect.

Mobile media. Sort of related to the first item. Someone has to imagine all of those programs and apps for phones, MP3 players, digital tablets and other devices that we didn't know we couldn't live without.

Occupational health and safety. Everybody wants to work in a safe, healthy environment. Somebody's got to figure out what that means—and enforce the rules.

English translation and foreign languages. The verbal currency of business worldwide is English. If you can combine excellence in English with translational skills in other languages (Spanish and Chinese come to mind), you're talking about possessing some truly marketable skills.

English as a foreign language. Speaking of English, why not teach it overseas? The demand for English-speaking teachers willing to venture abroad is huge. Walshok and colleagues say that "by 2015 half the world's population will be speaking Shakespeare's favorite lingua franca."

Renewable energy and green jobs. Maybe you're sick of hearing about it, but green jobs really are an evergreen opportunity, from developing electric cars, solar panels and wind farms to figuring out how to protect and preserve the only planet we have.

Action sports innovators. Snowboarding is an Olympic sport. Skating and surfing are billion-dollar industries. Somebody has to design, make and sell all of the related merchandise. Not to mention invent the next big thing. Welding, pipe fitting and mechanics. Okay, these jobs don't sound as exciting as designing the next electric car or creating a single board that surfs, skates and sails, but both of those creations are bound to surface. Along with all our more mundane inventions. When that happens, who are you going to call?

Independent consulting. People go to work for big companies because they offer paid vacations and health and retirement benefits. Well, they used to. Many of those perks have been pared back, maybe eliminated altogether. If that's the case, what's the point of working for someone else when you can work for yourself? Independent consulting is a pretty vague term, but also enticing. It just means that if you have a marketable expertise, you can probably use it to your benefit. People and companies are usually willing to pay for specific knowledge, especially if they don't also have to pay for vacations and benefits.

Geriatric healthcare. Let's face it, we're all getting older. And this year marks the first big wave of Baby Boomers hitting retirement age. In time, we're all going to need a little—or a lot of—help.

phil•osophy 101

4

The 10/90% theory.

I spent much of my childhood living abroad. My father worked in the petroleum industry. In the 1960s, the quickest way to boost one's career was to volunteer for work overseas. Many of my father's colleagues were content to stick to the States, but not him. Folks thought he was crazy to leave the comforts of Oklahoma, to take his young family to foreign countries, but my father was ambitious. When a new oil field was discovered in, say, Venezuela, he would be sent there to open up offices. We, of course, went along. My father didn't love the job, but it paid well and he had a family to support. That's how it worked in those days.

For a kid it was an "interesting" life. We never stayed in a place more than a few years. I was shy. I started at a new school every few years, usually appearing in the middle of a semester. I attended elementary school in Caracas, Venezuela, and junior high in Tripoli, Libya. I was always the kid who walked into a classroom and was introduced by the teacher as "the new student." I never really got into team sports, probably because by the time I usually arrived, teams had been organized and positions taken. Everybody else seemed to know each other. It took time to make friends, become part of the scene and often, when that finally happened, it was time for my family to move again.

My mother was a big driver in my family. My parents were both hearty Midwestern stock. They had strong, conservative values and an exceptional work ethic. Dad went off to work. Mom remained home, though she had too much energy to just clean and bake. As soon as my older brother and I reached high school, she got a job too, which was a pretty rare thing in the 1960s. My parents' work ethic rubbed off on my brother and me.

Sitting around the house watching TV wasn't an option for either of us. If I wasn't going to keep busy with school and sports, then she figured I might as well be productive and do some odd jobs. So I mowed lawns, shoveled snow, sold pens and stationery, babysat. Mom always drove me wherever I needed to be. She was very empowering.

When you're a small business person (and I was, both in size of business and stature), you meet a lot of people. You learn how to carry on a conversation with adults; how to develop your business. I negotiated prices for weekly lawn services and snow shoveling after storms. The clients were several times my age, but I think I held my own. I became comfortable talking to, and negotiating with, people much older and more powerful than me.

I discovered, mostly unconsciously, that the more people I talked to, the richer I became. Not necessarily in money, but knowledge. Everybody has a story to tell. Everybody can teach you something. It might be practical information, like how to write a contract. Or it might be personal, like how to start up a conversation with a stranger. I've learned something from virtually everybody I've ever met. Sometimes what to do and sometimes what not to do. And the fun is I'm still learning.

I am convinced that life is 10% what happens to you and 90% how you choose to react to what happens. Two people can see a troublesome situation and one falls on their sword immediately, sees it as the worst thing to ever happen, gives up, and suffers the consequence. The other person takes the problem on as a challenge, works through it, and learns from it. Which kind of person are you and which kind of person do you want to be?

I have never understood the attraction of falling on the sword. I thrive on being around positive, upbeat people. People who see the cup half-full are, in fact, my favorite people. Have you met people that for some reason you just like being around? You feel better about yourself when you are in their presence? They are happy people. They find good things to say about other people. They laugh at themselves. They never take life too seriously. And they bring you out of yourself and make you an active part of their conversation or activity. They continually stretch and test themselves. They give you the confidence to do the same.

Equally important, upbeat people are rarely critical of other people. They understand other people's weaknesses, and always try to help them through an issue. They even go out of their way to find the positive in everyone. Upbeat people rarely complain about anything.

These are the kind of people I want to have in my posse! This is the kind of person I want to be and I want you to be.

I have a pet peeve: Sighing and moaning. Sue, a salesperson who is no longer with Manpower, had a habit of coming into my office and letting out the longest, loudest sighs as she threw herself in a chair across from me. When she sat down, she moaned. When she stood up, she moaned—as if it was the hardest thing she had done all day. After the second time she did it, I told her she sucked all the energy out of the room! I realize selling is a hard and often frustrating job. But don't take it out on the rest of us. As a salesperson, Sue needed to bring energy into a room, not draw it out. She realized the negative vibes and body language she had unconsciously been portraying and quickly changed.

I feel this way about loud yawns too. Yawns scream I am tired and/or bored. For whatever metaphysical reason, we all find yawns to be contagious. Someone yawns and the rest of us unconsciously follow suit. Not a good thing. If you have to yawn, stifle it as much as humanly possible. And don't be one of those people who yawns without covering your mouth. I have no interest in looking down your throat.

Don't forget—people are your greatest resource. It's easy and natural in hard times to withdraw into your cubbyhole, to hunker down and wait out the storm. I know it can be depressing and even embarrassing to be out of work when it seems like everyone else has a job. This is when you most need to reach out and touch someone, anyone, and everyone. That's what this chapter is all about and it's easier than you think.

Resources are everywhere

"A pessimist sees the difficulty in every opportunity; an optimist sees the opportunity in every difficulty."
— WINSTON CHURCHILL

"It's a recession when your neighbor loses his job; it's a depression when you lose your own."
— HARRY S. TRUMAN

"Nowadays joblessness isn't just for philosophy majors."
— KENT BROCKMAN

We Are All Temps

Even in the best of times, millions of Americans are unemployed.

And tens of millions more are just one bit of bad news away.

You will hear me say this more than once: "We're all temps." No one is a "permanent" employee. Our jobs exist only as long as our company needs our skill set, as long as we do the job better than someone else, as long as the company we work for is competitive and stays in business. This is the age of mergers and acquisitions—if another company buys or merges with your company, all bets are off. No matter how wonderful an employee you are, if you become redundant, you become expendable.

If that sounds pessimistic, it isn't. As hard as we try, we cannot dictate the direction of our work lives. There are factors beyond our control. And there always will be. All of which means, simply, that we're in this together, we're in the same boat rising and falling on the changing tides of commerce, economics, politics and life. If you're unemployed or worried about becoming so, know this: You're not alone.

I wrote this book for people who are facing one of life's tougher challenges. You can get through the tough times with positive persistence.

Just know the process can be arduous, even daunting.

When you are out of work or wanting to make a career change, everybody is a potential resource, everybody may be able to offer you guidance and assistance. Help is everywhere if you know where to look for it, how to access it, and what to do with it when you find it.

This chapter is all about finding, creating and managing your resources.

Everybody is a resource. There are lots of organizations and groups, many long-established, whose expressed goal is to support people looking for a job. Some of the best will be highlighted here. More importantly, I'll explain what makes them effective and useful to you, and how you can best take advantage of their services.

Networking 101

Here's a word we'll use a lot: Networking.

Admittedly, it's a trendy verb that's overused. The relevant definition of "network" is "a group of interconnected or cooperating individuals." The best way to find a job in this economy, or any other, is by networking.

My goal is to give you solid, substantive tips on how to find, develop and manage a network of people that will lead you to the job of your dreams.

In this chapter you'll learn how to develop your group of networking contacts, and in Chapter 6, we will detail "informational interviews" that you will conduct with these friends and friends to be. They are gold to you. These interviews are your opportunity to tell others very clearly how they can help you in your job search.

According to various studies, almost 60% of all jobs are filled as a result of some level of networking. 50% of all jobs that are filled aren't even advertised. They are uncovered through word-of-mouth; someone telling someone else about an opportunity or about an individual they think would be perfect for a job. You need to be the person they are thinking of when they hear about an opening that is not right for them. To make that happen you have to meet lots of people and tell them the type of job you are look-ing for. That is networking. It's a personal skill that needs to be learned and practiced until it becomes as natural as taking a breath. It involves reaching out to family, friends, colleagues, acquaintances and most commonly, com-plete strangers to hear and learn about these unadvertised opportunities.

Networks have myriad uses:

- To find job leads,
- To discuss new directions,
- To generate career options,
- To problem-solve,
- To assess transferable skills,
- To sharpen a résumé for an interview,
- To hook up with role models or mentors;
- To simply receive emotional support.

But wait, you might say: "How can I network? I don't know anybody."

That's nonsense. Unless you've spent the last 20 years on a desert island or holed up in a mountain cave, you know people. They may not be associated with your dream company, but that doesn't matter. As you will soon learn, often someone you know knows someone else who knows someone else. Eventually, when done right, you will get to the person you need to get to.

Your network is only as good as the people you put in it or, more importantly, the people who can be brought into it. It's not just quantity, but quality. Knowing 1,000 people won't help if most of those 1,000 can't help you. But what you will soon learn is how to finesse the people you do know to use their networks to do reconnaissance work for you. And here's how you begin:

Finding, Developing and Managing Networks

As soon as you find out, either by your choice or someone else's, that you will be in the job search mode (maybe you've heard rumors of layoffs or you're just ready to make a move), alert every appropriate member of your networking group.

If you're looking for a job, now is no time to be shy. Don't hesitate to contact people you haven't seen for some time. Remember, they haven't been in contact with you either. Your effort to reach out may be much appreciated and welcomed. Think Facebook and LinkedIn. These are excellent methods to reconnect with lost acquaintances and both sites are easy to use.

Your job search network should be as expansive as possible. The more people you enlist, the better your chances for success.

In the employment/human resources industry, a compilation of one's networking contacts is sometimes known as the "Christmas card" list. Typically, it's 50 or more individuals whom you can count on for support and guidance. You may already have such a list. If you do not, here are some suggested sources for creating one:

- Neighbors, current and former
- Employers, current and former
- Co-workers, current and former
- Friends
- Family members
- Past teachers and professors
- Members and clergy from your church or religious institution
- College alumni (think about contacting your alma mater's career center too)
- Social acquaintances, such as exercise partners or sports teammates
- Salespeople you've done business with
- People who have provided services, such as hair stylists or mechanics
- Fellow volunteers from charity work
- Classmates from any grade level
- Politicians, including local city council and school board members
- Doctors, dentists, lawyers and accountants
- Business club members (e.g., Rotary, Lion's Club)

I have no idea whose research resulted in this number, but the lore of career counseling says that unless you have an active "Christmas card" list of at least 89 people then you should not consider a direct sales position like insurance, financial planning or consulting. The point they want to make is that you are not a natural communicator if you don't actively keep in touch with that many people. Regardless of the validity of this number, it is an interesting concept. After you've compiled potential members for your network, prioritize it while keeping in mind the attributes of a good contact:

- The person likes you or has reasons to help you. They have a personal or professional investment in your success and well-being.
- The person knows a wide range of people who are "plugged in." These are connections that can be useful to you.
- The person is savvy about the existing job market and future employment trends. Their knowledge has real currency and value.
- The person is successful in his or her own career. This is evidence they know what they're talking about.

Be very clear about what you are seeking from networking contacts. Be professional and appropriate. Don't ask (or worse, insist) that people do things they may not be comfortable doing, or cannot do without extraordinary effort, or that may damage their reputations. An example might be asking them to make an introduction to the HR staff at the company where they work. They just might not feel like they know you well enough. If you sense someone is balking at any request you make, graciously pull back and try another approach.

You want your network of contacts to be a living, growing, enduring entity. You'll need and want to be able to go back to your contacts from time to time (remember: no job is permanent; careers change, we are all temps), so long-term nurturing of these relationships is essential. Stay in touch. Keep people apprised of your job search progress and success. Send thank you notes for job leads or services rendered.

Sarah met with me for an informational interview; I was able to give her some hot leads, and good tips about how to avoid the black hole. After a nice thank you note, I never heard from her again. I wonder if she is still out there searching for a job. She is out-of-sight and therefore out-of-mind. I would have been a great person to put on that Christmas card list.

Robert, on the other hand, stayed in touch with regular updates (every three weeks or so). I felt like I was vested in his success because he cared enough to stay in touch with me. When I thought he was straying off target, I could shoot him a quick email. When he was sounding discouraged, I could share some encouragement. Most important. when he got the job of his dreams, I could congratulate him and share in his joy. Next time Robert needs my advice or input, I will be happy to hear from him. Sarah, on the other hand, not so much.

Managing a network can quickly become overwhelming if you don't stay organized. Create a notebook or database to keep track of all of your contact names and networking activities. Document whom you spoke with, the topics discussed and the projected outcomes. Check off who (everyone) you've sent thank you notes to and what you discussed. Diligently file all correspondence, including notes and emails, so that you can quickly retrieve them as needed. See my website, job-won.com, for a sample of how to manage this process.

One caveat: Don't tell the world about your job search.

Just as an employer has no obligation to inform employees that their jobs are at risk, you're under no obligation to tell your employer that you've begun a new job search. In most states, employees work "at will." That grants employers and employees tremendous flexibility. As an employer, it means I need only employ you as long as I have need for your particular skills, and you need only do that job as long as you desire to be employed by me. There's a lot more legalese to it, but that's the bottom line.

Just as an employer can consider downsizing you out of a job, you can ponder leaving the company—and it's nobody's business but your own.

I recommend you do not broadly announce your potential departure plans to your current employer or co-workers. Be selective about whom you share your plans with. If possible, don't even tell your closest colleagues unless you trust them implicitly and they are an essential part of your network. Co-workers can be some of your best allies since they know your work habits and talents better than anyone else, or they can rat you out to the boss if they covet your job. The last thing you want is an early dismissal from your current position.

If an employer hears that you are looking for a job elsewhere, it is reasonable for them to begin to envision the company without you. You've opened the door to the possibility of leaving. Your employer may decide to push you through that door earlier than you want. So keep your plans to yourself as much as possible.

As you network with people, it is also very appropriate to explain that you are still working at your current employer and would appreciate their discretion.

Ron had a heart-to-heart conversation with his boss about not getting the raise he expected and unfortunately blurted out "Well maybe I'll have to start looking elsewhere." The die was cast. The employer felt the lack of commitment and at the next "resizing" Ron was the first to be let go. Be careful that your mind is in gear before your lips start moving and make comments you will later regret.

One more thing: As long as you're employed, respect your employer. It's not fair or ethical to actively seek another job during work hours. Your employer is paying you for that time and deserves your full attention. Earn your paycheck every day. Use personal time off, vacation time or take a day off without pay to pursue your job search. Lunchtime can be very productive for returning calls or doing interviews. Also be cautious using your company email address. No telling who sees those emails since they legally belong to the company. Plus it just feels wrong. It is very easy to get a new email address to use solely for job search issues.

How you conduct your job search speaks volumes to potential employers. If you're busily pursuing a new job on company time, other companies will assume you would do the same with them. Not a good way to start an interview.

Bill was fed up with where he was working. Whether he had valid reason for these strong feelings is irrelevant. He badmouthed his current employer at every opportunity. When he interviewed, he called in sick or disappeared from work for long stretches of time. Worse, he bragged during interviews about how he felt no guilt interviewing during work time. He felt they owed him that. As far as I know, Bill is still looking for a job.

ORGANIZATIONS AND HOW TO USE THEM

Effective networking happens all of the time, anytime, anywhere. It's important to always be prepared. One sign of being prepared is having business cards on hand.

A business card is really an old fashioned "calling card." It need not be elaborate and, in fact, probably shouldn't be. The card should bear your name and basic contact information, like name, phone number and email. That's it. Don't include things like your home address. Where you live is nobody's business. I have seen business cards with the job seeker's 30 second elevator speech printed on the back. Interesting approach to consider if you are set on your job focus.

Check out Vanityprinting.com for free business cards.

Carry these business cards with you at all times. Don't leave home without them. They are a sign of your professionalism and a key to opening many doors. And carry them in some sort of protective case. It is bad form to hand someone a bent, dirty, lint-covered card. Scrounging around for a pen and tearing pieces of paper off to write your contact information on is not a good start for a new contact.

Jake was a client at a recent speaking engagement. I had just mentioned the importance of professional business cards when his hand popped up. "I don't have a job," the man said. "How can I have a business card?" That's no excuse.

There are many venues specifically tailored to networking opportunities and contact exchanges, such as job fairs, civic conventions, trade shows, online user groups, bulletin boards and professional association meetings. Professional associations are among the most promising of opportunities. They are filled with avid networkers. In fact, that's one of their central functions.

With all of the high-tech tools available to job seekers, it's easy to spend an inordinate amount of time at your desk in front of a computer monitor. I got a very indignant email from Mary Lou (I changed the name to protect the guilty), a TV viewer who pointed out that in the last two years she had sent out 2,000 résumés, and had been in front of her computer for eight to ten hours a day and only had four interviews. This was bad on lots of levels. She was mad at me and turned off a potentially good contact. She obviously was not customizing her résumés for every job, and how can you meet people sitting at home in front of your computer? Get out and meet real people, people who can make things happen for you.

Professional associations offer face-time with people who can provide behind-the-scenes insights into different companies and industries. They also are the most likely to know about the "hidden job market." Look for association meetings relevant to your job or career interests. One good place to start is by visiting the American Society of Association Executives at asaecenter. org. Most professional association web sites post industry news, job trends, resource libraries, membership directories and calendars of upcoming meetings. More importantly, they often post job openings in their "Career" sections.

Attend a meeting, either as a guest or become a member, if the cost isn't prohibitive. These gatherings are rich in potential contacts and employment opportunities. They can be high-energy and inspiring, motivating you even more. They also usually have speakers that you may find of interest.

Don't be surprised to discover other people looking for jobs at these meetings. They are attending the meeting for the same reason you are and may be competition, but they're a support too. Other job seekers are a great resource for learning about positions and possibilities that might otherwise slip by unknown. In a sense, your network is tapping into their networks. They can tell you about jobs that were not right for them but might be right for you. Just remember to be equally considerate: Share information and tips freely. Be generous. Pay it forward. Acts of kindness always pay off. People will remember.

Keep in mind, networking can happen anywhere. Networking occurs in restaurants and bars, in continuing education classes, at parties, on a bus, train or airplane, in an online chat room, at a sporting event, kids soccer games, volunteer activities or fundraisers. The way I see it, every moment you're not asleep can be a networking opportunity.

Elevator Speech: Don't Leave Home Without It

You don't activate a network simply by calling the first name on your contact list on Monday morning. First you have to develop a plan. Or more precisely, a good, solid idea of what kind of job you're looking for and how you hope your network contacts can help.

How can other people, no matter how well they know you, give you advice about career paths if you have no clue about what you are looking for? Step one is putting your thoughts, no matter how undeveloped, down on paper. This is the beginning of your "elevator speech," a smooth, persuasive 30-second pitch describing yourself and explaining your career goals. The name is a reference to the amount of time it typically takes to ride an elevator. The pitch is your answer to a question you'll likely hear again and again from contacts and potential employers:

"What kind of work are you looking for?"

It's a straightforward query, but fraught with peril. An effective elevator speech gets your foot in the door, verbally speaking. A poor speech gets it closed in your face.

A solid elevator speech presents you and your plans clearly, compellingly and, most of all, concisely. No one wants to hear a long, rambling dissertation. There is great power and persuasion in brevity.

Need proof? Consider this:

Abraham Lincoln's address at Gettysburg in 1863 is considered one of the finest, most memorable speeches of all time. Yet it consists of fewer than 300 words and was delivered by Lincoln in less than three minutes.

By contrast, the marquee speech that day was given by a noted orator named Edward Everett, whose commentary was also originally called "the Gettysburg Address." Everett's oration was 13,607 words long. It took him more than two hours to deliver. No one today remembers what he said.

Over the years, I've heard plenty of elevator speeches, some that made me wish I could get off the elevator before my floor and even a few that made me wish I could just jump out a window, however many floors up.

There is no single, perfect elevator speech. They are always a work in progress. What works in one situation might not in another. You will have a different elevator speech for every career twist and turn. You will need to adjust it as things change. But beyond brevity, here are a few key requirements:

- Your introduction should be memorable. Clever and witty are good.
- It should be easy to understand. Avoid industry jargon. Be clear. Don't leave the listener wondering what you mean.

- Emphasize one or two of your particular strengths or talents. Set yourself apart. Let people know why they need to know more about you.
- Make sure you tell your listener how to learn more about you. Ask about getting together. Give them a business card.

Here's a scenario: You're actually in an elevator, doors open, when someone you know steps in and says hello, followed by the usual "How are you?" One choice is to simply say "fine." End of conversation. But here's a different ending (and maybe a beginning too):

You: Hi Alan, thanks for asking. I'm doing well. I'm in the process of looking for a new job.

Alan: Really. What kind of job?

You: I'm looking for a position in the international telecommunications industry where I can put my MBA and 10 years experience at Nokia to work at a company like Qualcomm, AT&T or Verizon. Hey, if you hear of anything, here's my card. In fact, do you mind if I follow up to share my career plans and get your opinion on several options I have?

Alan: Not at all. Here is my card.

This imagined conversation is not far-fetched. It can easily happen, and pay off in spades, provided you're prepared, recognize the moment and seize it. In this case, it was a chance to tell Alan about your availability and give him a quick, informative run-down of what you're looking for in a new job. Specifically, what information did you impart?

- You're looking for a new opportunity.
- Your particular job interest is international telecommunications, especially with a company like Qualcomm, AT&T or Verizon.
- You have 10 years of experience at Nokia.
- You have an MBA.
- You respect his advice and input.

That's a lot accomplished on an elevator ride. Alan (or anybody else on the elevator) might not be able to help directly, but he might know someone else who can. They have become members of your working network and you have set yourself up for the all-important informational interview.

Abraham Lincoln was a polished, consummate speaker. The man knew how to communicate in ways that transcended the moment. Unless you have Lincolnesque abilities, you will have to practice your elevator speech until you have it down cold. You may find yourself giving it at any moment—maybe even in an elevator—so practice and constantly look for ways you can improve upon it. Listen for persuasiveness, content and clarity. Don't speak too quickly or resort to slang. You don't want to sound stilted or scripted. Try it out on friends. They may have useful tips.

Also be aware that as we develop career paths that you will have different elevator speeches for each one. The example above is for telecommunications. You may also have one for electronics and facility maintenance if those are also areas of interest. Knowing which elevator speech to give on impulse is a bit tricky.

Make Job Fairs Work for You

Job fairs are obvious opportunities for networking, but they require thought and preparation. The fairs, which bring together many companies and potential employers under one roof, at one time, are valuable one-stop career shops.

Job fairs occur all the time, but you may have to go looking for them. Search the internet, newspapers, college career centers and employment agencies for announcements of upcoming fairs. Select those that feature companies and careers that interest you. You will also have an opportunity to talk to large companies that are from out of town. Relocation is always the 800-pound gorilla in the room, but may always be an option, even internationally.

A job fair isn't a job interview, but it's close. You must go prepared. Begin by reviewing your career strengths as described in your résumé and identified in your earlier self-assessment. Practice introducing yourself and delivering your elevator speech. Be prepared to confidently discuss your career achievements, not your job duties, with potential employers.

Dress as you would for a real job interview (more on that in Chapter 5.) Bring numerous copies of your résumé. If you do well, you'll hand out a lot of them. You will want to write up a general cover letter to attach to your résumé, a summary that clearly defines your career objectives and qualifications in relation to the relevant industry or focus of the job fair. Strong, succinct cover letters make a positive impression. In my experience, few job fair attendees take the time and effort to write and distribute these letters, so doing so will help set you apart from the masses. It shows you put more effort into preparing for the fair than hundreds of others attending. Already, you stand apart.

Chris, a friend of a friend, is a high-level executive who stood in line for two hours just to get into the room where the recruiting booths were located. This is no time to wear your ego on your sleeves. Be patient, chat with the people in front and behind you. They are in the same outrageous line so make the best of the situation. Know that they feel the same way you do and it's just part of the cost of admission. That's also why it is so important that you be prepared when you talk to the recruiters so that you make the most of your time and theirs. The recruiters will be grateful too.

By the way, Chris got a great lead from someone while standing in line that made it all worthwhile.

Keep your materials neat, organized and presentable in a handheld portfolio that allows you to easily shake hands with potential employers and take notes.

Don't forget to bring along an abundance of your business cards. Notepad, pen and your calendar are also essential, the last in case a prospective employer wants to arrange a meeting or interview on the spot.

Do some research ahead of time when you know which companies will be represented at a job fair. Check out corporate websites, keying in on any job openings of interest that are posted. Read current, relevant news. Doing so will make conversation easier and more effective with company representatives. Asking intelligent, informed questions about such topics as the company's recent accomplishments or future plans sets you apart from the other unprepared looky-loos...tire kickers as I call them.

View your job fair interactions as seriously as you would a job interview. On-site job fair interviews are, in fact, becoming much more common. It makes sense. The candidate and the recruiter are both there, so why not have an introductory interview? It saves everybody time and money. Don't be surprised if a seemingly casual conversation evolves into something more serious and you are asked to sit down for a formal interview. Always appear flexible, but never desperate.

Following up with recruiters and new contacts at a job fair is more than just an afterthought. How and when you follow up leaves as much of a lasting impression on potential employers as your on-site interview or conversation does. Maybe more so since it underscores your seriousness, determination and professionalism. You are fighting to get this job.

The *day after* a job fair, send a cover letter expressing your interest, a fresh résumé and a personalized note of thanks to each promising corporate contact. Remind the contact of your recent job fair meeting and your relevant career qualifications. Remember they probably met hundreds of people that day so make yourself stand out if you possibly can by mentioning something unique about your conversation.

I have worked many a job fair in my time. You meet hundreds of people in a day and they all become blurs. You will usually see a table behind the recruiters where they collect résumés. When they/we turn to set down your résumé, there are subtly three stacks going. A "yes" stack, a "maybe" stack and a "no chance" stack. You can never tell if the rating is right to left or left to right. Guessing can make you crazy.

If you committed to calling an employer, do so, but leave no more than two messages. This is important. Leaving too many messages does not signify admirable persistence. If you've done your homework and made a good impression, a phone call or two simply punctuates a job search done well. Phone messages also give the recruiter an opportunity to test your phone etiquette and communications skills. Anything more begins to smack of desperation and becomes counterproductive.

I met with a young man named Ryan. He had a good résumé and presented himself well. Our informational interview went fine. I said I would be in touch, and I meant it.

The next day, the fellow left me a message expressing his thanks for talking with him and reiterating his eagerness to find work. The day after that, he called again—same message. And again, the next day and the day after that.

This was too much. I went from being happy to help to dreading his next, inevitable call. I wondered whether he was doing anything else to pursue his goals besides calling me. He started to feel more like a stalker than a prospective employee. And nobody hires stalkers!

Once you've sent your letters and thank you notes, once you've made your calls, be prepared to wait. Employers and human resources personnel work according to their schedules—needs and priorities that you are likely not privy to. You are not the only job seeker they are considering. Be patient. Use the time to pursue other job leads.

Also, priorities change. Whether a job fair or a job interview, I know it is very frustrating when the recruiter does not get back to you in what you consider a reasonable time. Here are the most likely reasons why:

- The decision makers are traveling
- After meeting with several candidates, the company is rewriting the job requirements
- A different job requirement has become more of a priority

You may not agree with their thinking, but at least you understand what could be going on behind the scenes that you don't see.

Effective Use of the Internet

Not so long ago, searching for a job meant pounding the pavement. It meant long days of actually knocking on doors and hoping for a face-to-face interview. The latter is still the goal, but the job search these days is often a lot easier on shoe leather.

Modern employers increasingly rely on the Internet to recruit talent, especially in certain competitive skilled labor markets such as engineering and software programming. They are looking for you as much as you are looking for them. That makes it paramount that you supplement your job search with keyword Internet employment searches and online résumé posting services. We keep talking about the importance of networking to find a job. Second best, and an area that must be covered, is putting your résumé up on the job boards. Never rely on job boards to find you a job, but also never ignore them. They are free and increase the odds that your résumé will be matched with compatible employers that are searching the job boards for employees with specific skills.

There are many resources online. Legitimate job search businesses, like Manpower, offer a wide variety of services, from massive job databases that are searchable by criteria from skills to salary, résumé clinics, cost-of-living calculators, networking exchanges, the latest interview trends and more.

Online job boards, however, are just one tool in your job search kit. In good times, posting your résumé on the web may prompt dozens of promising responses. In bad times, it might not solicit a single reaction.

The reason, of course, is competition. With millions of résumés circulating on the Internet, yours is likely to be a snowflake in a blizzard. According to one survey, the odds of getting a job through one of the big employment boards like Monster or CareerBuilder is less than two in 100.

And that's if you do it right. Limit the time you spend on job boards. No more than 20% of your search time should be spent in front of a computer. Computers don't hire people, people hire people. You can also tell the boards to notify you when a new job posting appears that matches your interests. The problem is they will be automatically notifying thousands of other job seekers too. Focus on and respond only to listings that closely match your skills, experience and interests. Unfortunately, the writers of job descriptions, the hiring managers and the HR department sometimes haven't communicated well and there is often disagreement about who is best for a position.

As a result, less than 1% of people who submit their résumés online for positions meet the actual criteria. Also know that as easy as it is for you to hit "submit", it is equally easy for HR to hit "delete." And once HR hits their delete button, your résumé goes into that really black hole. Make sure your résumé does show you are a valid candidate for the job. Don't provide employers with a quick and easy way to reject you, such as overlooking typos in your résumé.

One of the allures to online job posting and search is the ease in which it can be done. The odds may be greatly against success, but it takes relatively little effort to try.

There are some perils you should be aware of: Not all online job boards or services are legitimate. Some are come-ons for résumé spamming services or sales schemes. Some are corporate guises just to assess candidate pools, with no intention of filling any of the listed jobs.

Be very careful about the information you post or list on your résumé. Beware of identity thieves. Legitimate job posters do not ask for your Social Security number, marital status or credit card information. Many reputable job service companies sell your personal information to advertisers and other third parties. Another reason not to have your home address on your résumé. Keep that in mind.

Here are some job boards that I think you will find helpful and their specific strength.

SOME RECOMMENDATIONS FOR ONLINE JOB POSTING SITES

DirectEmployers.com   A nonprofit service that provides varied job postings garnered from corporate members.

Monster.com   Job seekers can execute keyword searches, post résumés, research job fairs and peruse career advice. The "Discover Your Passion" tool helps you link your interests to possible careers.

Indeed.com   A jobs-only search engine. Scans all current job listings from major job boards, newspapers, associations and company career pages.

CareerBuilder.com   Job-matching technology scans your résumé for keywords, remembers what you've searched for and collects details from jobs you've applied to.

SimplyHired.com   A simple, one-step search site. Up to 500,000 jobs identified by keyword, location or both.

Jobing.com   Résumé postings and job searches by city.

USAJOBS.gov   Official site of the U.S. government's Office of Personnel Management, a one-stop source for federal employment information.

Military-Jobs.com   Targets veterans, particularly those in high-tech fields.

Careerjournal.com   This is the Wall Street Journal's executive career site.

Onetcenter.org   A government site that helps you determine skills and education necessary for different occupations.

Quintcareers.com   Quint is short for quintessential. The site provides free college, career and job search content, plus tips, trends and coaching.

Rileyguide.com   A useful A-Z index of job-hunting websites and services. It doesn't post jobs or résumés, but points you to places that do.

LinkedIn.com   More than 120 million professionals use LinkedIn to exchange information, ideas and opportunities.

Craigslist.com   Widely used, no frills bulletin board for job opportunities.

CORPORATE INVESTIGATIONS

I'm not talking about cloak-and-dagger stuff here or industrial espionage. Rather, you need to learn more about companies you'd like to work for, the targets of your aspirations and applications.

Obviously, the depth of your investigation will reflect the depth of your interest. Don't waste time on companies for which you have little interest. The first place to start is with the major search engines, such as Google, Bing and Yahoo. Search for information by company name, the names of top personnel and relevant keywords.

At the very least, you should be able to find a company's website, which ought to be a wealth of information, providing you with its organizational structure, the names of employees and a sense of how it sees itself and is seen by others.

If you've Googled to exhaustion and still want more, there are more specific sites that might be useful. Here are some:

Hoovers.com	A subscriber-based service that lists corporate information like top executives, annual sales, growth figures, competition, etc. You have to pay for much of this information, but just poking around can turn up a lot.
Vault.com	Also subscription-based, with much of the same material as Hoover's, but it also provides a peek at corporate cultures. There are surveys and message boards where people (including employees) can discuss prospects, culture, products and the like.
IndustryWeek.com	Provides free information on the top 1,000 manufacturing companies internationally and the top 500 in the United States.
BusinessWire.com	A comprehensive listing of news releases from thousands of companies and organizations.
Reportgallery.com	Links to more than 2,000 annual reports from major and mid-sized companies. Annual reports are a good way to see how a company wants the rest of the world to see it. And, if you know how to read them closely, they offer a wealth of information and data.

CorporateInformation.com   Requires free registration, but allows you to research thousands of companies, here and around the world.

Give.org   A go-to source for information on non-profit organizations consolidated by the Better Business Bureau. Its "charity reports" detail primary projects, budgets, staff and top personnel. A similar source is GuideStar.org.

COMPUTER LITERACY

Nearly every job or career today requires some level of computer literacy. What do you need to know? Generally speaking, employees are expected to possess a basic understanding of computer hardware and software, particularly word processing, spreadsheets, email and perhaps PowerPoint.

At the very least, you should be familiar with Windows operating systems and, if your field emphasizes graphics and design (such as marketing and advertising), Mac-based software applications. You must have a functional email account, and this should not be one you share with your husband or wife or the kids. You should know how to use basic Web browser functions, such as searching, bookmarking, history, refreshing, etc. You should know how to scan or upload photos, documents and other file types. You should be able to download software.

Odds are, most of these skills are already well-honed, but if they are not, consider enrolling in a computer education class at your local community college or career center. Bring your abilities up to date and add new ones. The more computer skills you have, the more competitive and attractive a job candidate you become. If your skills are limited or rusty, you obviously have the time now to work on them. One way to impress prospective employers is to discuss the new skills you have developed during your "down" time. You now have a history of making good use of your time.

Unless you are applying for an administrative job, do not list basic computer skills like Microsoft Word, Excel and PowerPoint. For management applications, it makes you sound like clerical rather than management material.

phil•osophy 101

5

This is the perfect place to stop and talk about paying it forward. We recently had the honor of dedicating the Manpower Lobby at San Diego Hospice in honor of a dear friend of the Katz and Blair families who passed away after receiving great care from the hospice. When we were touring the hospice building, we were struck by how all of the naming opportunities were family names. There were no corporate sponsors. Hospice has always been generously supported with gifts from families in honor of their loved ones. As a big believer in cause marketing—the use of marketing dollars to support nonprofits rather than just philanthropic dollars (which are drying up quickly)—we decided to name the lobby under our corporate name. In my comments at the luncheon, I told the crowd that as corporate leaders, we need to think about paying it forward by supporting services that our employees need now rather than after their need of service.

In fact, within one month, a Manpower staff person was sitting in the hospice lobby, checking in her very ill mother, when she looked up and realized that the company she worked for was a tangible hospice supporter. She couldn't find the words to describe how proud she was of the company where she worked.

This is a long way to get to the importance of "paying it forward" in our personal life and in our job searches. The friend who called his father on my behalf when I was looking for work was doing me a big favor with no expected payback. You can be assured I will forever go out of my way to share any contacts I have and to support him in any way I can when he asks or needs assistance.

During your job search, go out of your way to help others, just as you would like them to help you. If you hear of an opportunity that's not right for you, stop and think about who it might be right for, and contact them immediately. That's paying it forward.

Phil

5 First steps

"When you come to a fork in the road—take it."
— YOGI BERRA

"Choose a job you love, and you will never have to work a day in your life."
— CONFUCIUS

"If opportunity doesn't knock, build a door."
— MILTON BERLE

Much of this chapter will make perfect, even obvious, sense when you read it. None of it should really be a surprise, but I repeat it here because it's critical to get the details right. When you don't, things can go sideways.

Even in tough job markets, there are—and will always be—job openings. Some will be widely publicized; most will not. In the latter case, it usually just takes a bit more work, a clever blend of resourcefulness and persistence, to uncover the "hidden job market."

So how do you go about finding the job that's right for you? Here is the abridged version, but still chockfull of nitty gritty details.

The Basics

First, there's the most obvious approach: You apply directly to an employer. Look for employers whose fields interest you, whose companies you admire and would want to pursue. Collect their addresses, phone numbers and websites. If you find something of interest, call the organization directly to inquire about their hiring process. Or better yet, visit the company with résumé in hand. If you don't have a contact name, ask to speak to a hiring manager or human resources representative.

Second, use your network. Ask every friend, relative, teacher, former co-worker and casual acquaintance whether they've heard about job openings. Tell them about your job search. This is no time to be bashful. Enlist them as scouts. The more people you have keeping an eye out and an ear to the ground, the more likely something will turn up.

Your "Christmas card" list is one place to start. Don't be afraid to ask for help. Someday you will be in a position to return the favor. Most people are happy to help.

Third, search the Internet. There are myriad job listing sites, bulletin boards and other places on the web that provide information and advertise positions. Indeed, the amount of information is staggering. But don't be daunted. Keep your search focused.

The converse of looking at jobs posted is to post your résumé online. Again, there are a lot of sites on the web offering this service and it's easy to get lost in the noise. This is where a smartly conceived and effective résumé is crucial, one that stands out in the crowd.

If you are still working, you will want to use sites like LinkedIn.com, where contacts are posted in a professional manner and citing career interests and opportunities doesn't necessarily scream job search.

Fourth, consider working for smaller companies. The commercial backbone of this country is the small business, not the giant conglomerates that dominate the news. Most new jobs are created by small, growing companies with fewer than 100 employees. Large employers are often more visible and aggressive in recruiting employees, but smaller companies often offer similar positions. Look for those that are expanding, with bright futures. They're often easier to approach than large corporations. When we finally dig ourselves out of this economic recession, it will largely be due to the thousands of small businesses who have hired the many, rather than the big companies hiring the few.

Fifth, explore temporary work. Aside from the fact that it may provide some much-needed income, temporary jobs can help you acquire experience, contacts and references. Temporary jobs often evolve into permanent opportunities. At Manpower, our customers hire 42% of our temporary associates. And many staffing companies, including Manpower, offer free training to boost career skills.

Sixth, contact any professional recruiter or executive search firm that you may know. This is a high-end, high-level option, one that's more often used if you have a specialized set of skills or advanced career experience. Recruiters tend to specialize in specific industries and skill clusters, such as finance, information technology, health care, technical writing or engineering.

The recruitment industry has changed much in recent years. The tough economy has made executive search firms (aka "headhunters") much more selective. These companies are paid a lot of money by companies to conduct a search to find the "needle-in-the-haystack" employee. Usually the company has been searching for months on its own, has not found a suitable candidate, is desperate because they needed the talent yesterday, and is willing to pay an executive search firm a very large fee.

As a result, executive search recruiters are usually not looking for (or taking calls from) unemployed job seekers, however talented. They prefer to troll for people who have jobs and who are not necessarily looking to make a change. The recruiter's task is to find a suitable target, then convince that person that the grass is much greener at the recruiter's client's company. This is why when we are asked to recommend a headhunter I have to explain that they are an icon of the past. Temporary firms like mine collect thousands of résumés for our database because we never know what skill sets we will need for the thousands of jobs we fill every year. An executive recruiter works on maybe three or four openings at a time.

If a recruiter contacts you, always hear them out. You never know what they might be offering of interest. Take their contact information, it just might come in very useful someday when you least expect it. They must have heard good things about you from someone to call you in the first place.

Seventh, check out newspaper classified ads, either print or online. Admittedly, their utility is diminishing fast. Only 25% of new jobs are found these days through newspaper ads, but they still remain an important place to visit and take the pulse of a local job market. Classifieds can give you a better sense of what's out there. They can also be a source of new ideas and inspiration. You may read about an interesting job, but at a company you have no interest in working for. At least you've discovered a new potential career path to research and pursue. Likewise you may see a job posting you are not qualified for but at a company you had not been aware of and want to research.

Finally, Google yourself. While you are doing research on prospects, add yourself to the list. Type in your name (plus a few other key search terms if you have a really common name) and see what kinds of results turn up. A lot of it might be irrelevant, but unless you've lived off of the grid without any connection to modern, technological society, there should be stuff about you on the web.

What does this stuff say about you? If the top item is an old news report about you streaking through a college football game back in the day, that's not good. Likewise, anything else that might portray you as something less than the fine, upstanding citizen you no doubt are. This is true for Facebook and LinkedIn pictures too. Just this week I had a client take down a picture from his Facebook page of him smoking a stogie: not exactly management material.

If you don't like your Google portrait, there are services that can help you get positive, professional links posted at the top of your search. You can't necessarily bury your past, but you can cloak it a bit.

Which brings up another point: Don't make things harder than necessary. In this era of Facebook, Twitter and social networking, it's fun and easy to post almost anything online: pictures of wild parties, random thoughts, etc. Once posted, these things are hard to retract later when you might regret having done them or let the world know.

Savvy employers look at Facebook pages. They read tweets. For them, these may be virtual revelations of the "real you," the side of you not polished and presented during a job interview. It's wise to scrub clean your social networking sites of any stuff that either no longer represents the person you are now, or which might prove embarrassing or hard to explain.

We HR managers are a suspicious people. What does it mean when you have a LinkedIn site but not a picture? Do you just not know how to follow instructions to upload a picture or are you ashamed to download your picture for the world to see? In this day of EEOC paranoia, we don't want to see a picture of applicants, but we kind of do. If an applicant does not have a site on LinkedIn or Facebook, what does that tell us? And, again, no picture on their site—what does that tell us?

You now have the basics of any job search. Do all of the above and you will be joining millions of other job seekers doing the same thing, looking for the same job at the same time. Now that you know the basics, let's move on to the reason you are reading this book and the techniques you should use for your job search that will set you apart from all others. Now it starts to get interesting.

Know the Product YOU'RE Selling

Know what it is that you have to sell before you go to market.

Let's work on what you really want to do in your career. What describes an acceptable job? And what defines an ideal job? If you don't know where you are going any road will do. Likewise if you don't know what makes you happy at work then you are doomed to fall into the bottom 50% of unhappy workers that we talked about earlier.

Let's start with what you love to do—what really makes you happy and feeling satisfied at the end of the work day? What would you do for free if you had the opportunity? You're likely to spend about 30% of your life, much of your waking existence, in the workplace, so it's critical that you truly enjoy your job. Anything less and your quality of life will suffer, as will the quality of life of everyone around you: family, friends, co-workers and employers.

Below is another schematic (also found on Job-Won.com). It consists of four columns labeled Love to Do, Like to Do, Willing to Do and Won't Do. The goal here should be obvious: To put into black-and-white exactly what you want in a job and what you do not. Be as realistic as possible in filling out this form. If there are job duties that you would prefer to avoid at all costs, such as public speaking, sales or extensive travel, now is the time to lay them all out there.

Example:

Love to Do	Like to Do	Willing to Do	Hate to Do
Write press releases	Ad copy	Research	Proof read
Interviews	Interview others	Background info	Memos
_____	_____	_____	_____
_____	_____	_____	_____
_____	_____	_____	_____

Before you can sell yourself to a would-be employer, you need to know what exactly you're selling. Each of us is a unique combination of skills (innate and learned), plus life experiences. But while that may separate us from everybody else, it isn't often immediately obvious to a hiring manager, who may deal with dozens of talented, qualified applicants in a day. Always remember that to you, this could be the most important interview of your career, but to the HR person it may be the eighth of the day and they are beginning to go bleary-eyed. In large firms, the first interview or two are very basic fact-finding meetings. The HR staff cannot be knowledgeable about every skill set in the company. So while they are interviewing you for an electrical engineer position, they barely know enough key phrases to prompt answers from you. They are the gatekeeper, to make sure the candidate is hirable material if their specific skill set checks out when they interview with the specific department manager that is hiring.

Your Best Advantage

To stand out from other job applicants, it is essential to categorize and confidently present your skills to the best advantage. Typically, skills are divided into three main categories: transferable, job-related and personal (or adaptive).

Here's a homework assignment. Look at the schematic below. Duplicate it on a piece of paper or download the form from Job-Won.com.

Transferable Skills	Applied at the Workplace
■ communication	edited company newsletter
	gave new employee orientations
■	
■	
■	

Job-Related Skills	Applied at the Workplace
■ Excel spreadsheets	compiled monthly sales reports
■ PowerPoint	organized quarterly sales meetings
■	
■	

Personal Skills	Applied at the Workplace
■ enthusiasm	organized company's United Way campaign
■ dependability	rarely took sick days
■	
■	

Transferable skills are those that can be applied to a wide variety of jobs or endeavors, such as problem solving, communication, attention to detail or self-motivation.

Next, jot down your job-related skills, which are specific to that job such as: computer programming, software or engineering experience or operating a forklift.

Finally, write down your personal or adaptive skills. These skills are the attributes that, *in toto*, make you who you are. They are part and parcel of your personality, such as enthusiasm, punctuality, honesty, loyalty, dependability and attitude.

But don't just write down a list of glowing adjectives. Include after each an example of how that particular attribute has been applied in the workplace at past jobs in your career. This is good practice for future job interviews. Most likely you will be asked "behavioral questions" as a way to demonstrate your personal skills. (We'll come back to those behavioral questions later, but basically they begin with lines like "Tell me about a time when you....").

As with many other elements of your job search, this skills list is an evolving, changing entity. You will likely add skills as others point them out or you become aware of their value. Often, we take talents for granted because they come easy to us. Public speaking, for example, might be no more difficult for you than humming in the shower, but for many, they would rather have a root canal.

Now that you've described your various skills and abilities, let's take a look at the whole picture. Creating the right blend of skills and effectively, persuasively communicating them to potential employers is key to landing the job. While many skills are singular and often impressive, employers tend to prize people who are "the complete package." They have a breadth of talent, a pleasant personality (meaning I'd like to work with this person) and the ability to virtually guarantee success. My goal is to help you develop the talents necessary to present yourself as that complete package.

Okay, so far you've compiled a list of what you can do and how you've applied it to past jobs.

Attitude is Number One

"We hire for attitude, we train for skills." This has been Mel's and my mantra for thirty years.

To every job you bring two sets of skills: hard and soft. Hard skills are those talents and abilities you've acquired and learned, either in school or through experience. Soft skills are life skills, such as your energy level, sense of honesty, capacity to work well with others. In other words, attitude toward life.

No matter what the position you are applying for—entry level or senior executive—you want to appear positive, upbeat, capable and confident. You want to project the qualities of a leader, one who can energize and inspire co-workers.

Attitude is the most influential personality trait that you directly control. It is the trait that is noticed first and remembered longest. Impress people with your positive attitude and you're halfway to your goal. Companies can teach the basics of the job. They can't teach attitude.

I once saw a sign in front of a gas station that said, "Now hiring: Only people with smiles need apply."

Of course, it's not always easy to maintain a positive attitude. The road to a new job is bumpy. There will be dips. So take a moment on a regular basis to step back and evaluate yourself. Are you feeling down? Are you dwelling on the negative? If your honest response is yes or even maybe (or if others have commented that you seem depressed or negative), take some time off to refresh and regroup. The last thing you want to do is blow your interview because you weren't at the top of your game.

A job search should not be a 24/7, "don't-sleep-until-success" endeavor. That just produces mistakes and burnout. Intersperse your search with moments for yourself. Escape to the gym or to the movies. Pick up a book on the power of positive thinking or an inspirational tale. A few of my favorites are *Over the Top: Moving from Survival to Stability, from Stability to Success, from Sucess to Significance* by Zig Ziglar, *The 7 Habits of Highly Effective People: Powerful Lessons in Personal Change* by Steven Covey and *Follow Your True Colors to the Work You Love: The Popular Method for Matching Your Personality to Your Career* by Carolyn Kalil, but there are many other worthy titles.

It's important to avoid negative people. Surround yourself with folks who inspire and energize you, whether it's directly related to your job search or just part of your life. Nothing empowers you more than associating with enthusiastic, energized, can-do friends and associates. Their energy is contagious.

Résumés 101

A successful job search requires that you be able to communicate well, both verbally and in writing. The ability to compose correspondence is critical, whether it's a résumé, cover letter, email or thank you note. Long before you ever get to dazzle a would-be employer face-to-face, you have to impress them with your command of the written word. That means being clear and concise—and free of misspellings and grammatical errors.

Let's look at three key forms of correspondence: cover letters, résumés and thank you notes.

COVER LETTERS

A well-crafted cover letter is as important as one's résumé. It sets the tone for everything that follows. It is often an employer's first exposure to you, the basis of their first impression. Some HR people read the cover letter first and if intrigued move on to the résumé. I happen to be a start-with-the-résumé person, and if intrigued, I move on to read the cover letter.

Either way, it is your first chance to introduce yourself and explain why you're the right person for the job. That's a weighty burden. A cover letter should be brief and introductory, neither a synopsis of your job history nor a lengthy dissertation.

A good rule of thumb is to keep a cover letter to just three paragraphs. The purpose here is to pique an employer's interest, provide a glimpse of your business writing talents, and of course, work towards getting an interview.

When writing a cover letter, avoid describing your personal attributes with terms like "assertive" and "highly motivated." Rather, list career accomplishments that demonstrate appealing skills and character strengths. Don't *tell* the potential employer that you're a hard worker who gets results. *Show* them.

Let's break down those three paragraphs:

Paragraph #1: In the first line or two, clearly identify the position you are seeking. You don't want the reader trying to guess your intentions. They won't bother. You should note where and how you learned of the job opening. Hopefully, you can reference someone known by the recipient of the letter. Be straight and to the point. You want the hiring manager or initial person deciding the fate of your application to know exactly where to direct your letter.

Here's an example:

Dear Ms. Smith:

At the suggestion of Rick O'Connell, I'm writing to apply for the position of Junior Manager in the carbonized peas department at Acme Farms Inc. Rick is the director of processing at Whole Planet Cogs & Wheels, a colleague and mentor. He thought we might be a good match. As a long-time admirer of Acme, I'm eager to explore that possibility.

Paragraph #2: This paragraph demonstrates that you can get the job done. It is a bridge connecting the job skills listed on your accompanying résumé with the requirements of the available position. Information that you might include here are details of related jobs, assignments or accomplishments, similarities to your current or most recent position and an explanation of why you believe you would excel at the job.

But don't stop there. Back up your points with quantifiable proof of your success and achievements, such as numbers, statistics, programs established and the like.

One technique is to compare listed requirements of a position with your particular experience. To wit:

At Whole Planet, I oversee the small pegs division. I'm responsible for a 20-person team that creates, markets and sells more than 1.2 million small pegs each year, bringing Whole Planet more than $5 million in revenue annually.

I've been with Whole Planet for six years, starting as an apprentice on the production floor where I learned the basics of manufacturing processes and systems. I have since pursued a rigorous program of professional development and improvement, with current licenses in online marketing and multi-platform distribution and a credential in quick-count carbonization.

Paragraph #3: In this final paragraph, deliver your closing pitch. Confidently restate your interest in the job and thank the potential employer. Be sure to request the next step in the employment process—an interview. Include information about how best to contact you to schedule a meeting or interview. Perhaps repeat your phone number and email address.

Here's an example:

Like Rick, I think I'm a good fit with Acme. I look forward to discussing with you soon how my background and experience can benefit your company. I hope it will be convenient for you if I call at 10:00 a.m. on Tuesday the 12th. I can be reached via email anytime at your-name@email.com or by phone at (555) 555-1234. Thank you again for your time and consideration. I look forward to hearing from you.

You will notice that the applicant took responsibility for making the first initiative. You don't want to put the burden on HR because while they may be impressed with your qualifications, your cover letter and references may get buried in a pile on their desk.

CREATIVITY OF RÉSUMÉS

Putting together a strong, persuasive résumé can seem a bit like trying to write the Magna Carta, especially the first time. Especially if it's the first time in a long time.

Résumés, of course, are those brief, written summaries of who you are as a person and why you are the right candidate for the job. They introduce you to potential employers. They outline your career accomplishments and work objectives, your qualifications, skills and experience. Their intent is to get the would-be hiring managers interested and curious enough (or better yet, excited enough) to want to meet you, to learn more about you, and, ideally, how you might fit into their organization or company. You want HR to have enough information to want to meet you; a résumé is not meant to be the sole contact that results in a job offer.

Still, that's a lot to pack into a document that should not exceed two pages. A résumé isn't the story of your life. I want you to refer to accomplishments, not duties. It's the story of your career and work history. It is a living document. It will change and evolve as you do, not just to reflect how your career has progressed, but also highlight your appropriateness for every job that seriously interests you. That's why I keep repeating that you have to develop a résumé for every single job that interests you.

For example, a professional writer exploring different kinds of careers would have different résumés for potential jobs in different arenas, from journalism to public relations to copywriting. Though he or she may possess skills that are common and crucial to all of these kinds of writing, different résumés will highlight those skills and experiences that are especially valued in particular kinds of work.

Résumé flexibility and multiplicity are important even if you're applying for several jobs at several companies, all of them roughly similar. It is essential to individualize each résumé to each job at each company, by highlighting specific experiences or talents that are important to that particular job at that particular employer. Every job opening you seriously pursue requires a cover letter and résumé designed specifically for it.

For example, let's say you're pursuing marketing jobs at two different companies. Both jobs are broadly similar, but Company A is looking for someone with exceptional "people skills" while Company B needs someone who's a master of numbers and finance. Your résumé should be tweaked to highlight your relevant talents and value to each company. While doing this, you are downplaying skills and experience that are not relevant to the designated job. You are doing HR a favor by not making them weed through data that they don't really care about. You are not lying or misleading the reader. If you have other skills that you think should be pointed out, do so. Never make the hiring manager labor to find reasons to interview you.

As you review your résumé(s), ask yourself whether the document makes you feel proud and accomplished. If the answer is no, there's more work to be done. If *you* aren't impressed with your résumé, no one else will be.

■　　■　　■

I can always tell when candidates are really serious about a particular job opening. If I advise them to rework their résumé to be specific to that opening and they balk, that's a red flag that they're not very serious. If they struggle to rework the résumé to display vital abilities and strengths key to getting a certain job, then maybe that job really isn't a job for which they are qualified– yet. If either of these cases applies to you, don't waste your time or the HR person's. Rethink and reset your target.

ANATOMY OF A RÉSUMÉ

A résumé represents you on paper; it's your body of work and more. The particulars will be unique, but the basic components are universal. I am not going to go into great detail about the basics for résumés, because you don't need me for that. Google "résumé preparation" and you will find lots of résumé writing sites that I think you will find very useful.

Let's get into the idiosyncrasies of résumés that HR professionals do notice.

Contact information: At the top of any résumé, place your first and last name, city of residence, applicable phone numbers and email address. You might notice I did not advise putting your complete home address, but only your city. Email and cell phones are the primary modes of communication these days. Few employers are going to write you a letter. Fewer still are likely to drive by your home to see if the weeds are pulled and the lawn mowed. So why do they need your home address?

I don't want to sound paranoid, but such information in the wrong hands can only spell trouble. HR departments don't want any more personal information about you than they actually need.

If you have what you think is a cute and clever email address, change it now. Stonedallday@gmail.com does not get you points. HR professionals don't think it's cute for employees to have the poor taste to have risqué email addresses and phone messages. It's very unprofessional.

Make certain to list phone numbers where you can definitely be reached. If you list a cell phone, always answer professionally. I know a fellow who always answers his cell phone with "Hellooooooooo." It sounds like he's testing out an echo chamber. It's endearing (sort of), but doesn't make him sound like a serious job candidate.

If you list a home phone number, use a reliable answering machine or voicemail system with a professional message that includes your full name, not just your phone number. Don't use your kids to record an adorable message. An employer is calling you and expects a professional exchange, not a cute exchange with your children.

If necessary, talk to family members or roommates to make sure they take detailed messages—and remember to give them to you so that you can reply in a professional, timely manner.

WHAT'S YOUR NAME AGAIN?

Use the name you prefer to be addressed by on your résumé. Seems like a logical request. If you have gone by Craig, your middle name, for the last 10 years, why do you put Robert on your résumé? Interviewers don't want to have to guess what name to call you. It's embarrassing when you have to correct us, either in the interview or weeks later. If you prefer "Craig" to "Robert", say so, as in Robert "Craig" Smith. If everybody knows you as "Bobbo," stick with just Craig Smith. Future colleagues will have plenty of time to learn your favorite fun-guy moniker after you've been hired. And maybe you should consider staying with Craig during the working hours and save Bobbo for drinking buddies.

If you are just out of college, do you want to start your professional career as Danny, Billy or Sissy? If you're asking my opinion—and since you're reading this book, I assume you are—I think not. This is the time to turn your childhood name into its adult version. I have trouble hiring a 50-year-old senior management person who professionally goes by Billy, or B.J. or Bambi. Does senior management really want to introduce its Vice President of Acquisitions as Timmy? Would Tim make a better first impression? When we grow up, I think our names should grow up with us.

If your name is difficult to pronounce, write it phonetically underneath or beside the first use. You want to avoid any awkwardness on the employer's side. If the employer feels like they might mispronounce your name or aren't sure what name you prefer to go by, they might avoid the entire situation by simply not using your name at all. This can sometimes mean not contacting you at all. And if you are in an interview, why make it awkward for someone to spend an hour with you without ever using your name?

OBJECTIVE ON YOUR RÉSUMÉ

Putting objectives on résumés is very subjective. Personally I like to see them. It makes my job much easier. Right at the top of your résumé it tells me the kind of job you are looking for and how well it matches the job I am working to fill. Hard to argue with that, isn't it?

A well-done objective is brief, specific and straightforward. It describes the position or career you seek, shows me how it matches well with my job description, but is broad enough to encourage readers to consider you for related jobs or opportunities.

Your goal here is to define:

■ Your areas of interest; e.g., the types of positions you seek and the skills you will use.
■ The type, size and scope of the organization you want to work for, whether international conglomerate or mom-and-pop shop.
■ The position level you seek: entry, supervisor, etc.
■ Your objectives. Keep these reasonable, real and honest. Vague platitudes and outrageous ambition are never helpful. If you are applying for a specific job closely reflect the potential job in the objective. This is where you can help the résumé reviewer come to the conclusion that you're a natural match for the position. For example, the position you are interested in is "AT&T is seeking a Senior Vice President of Sales and Marketing for its Latin American market. Ideal candidate to have 10 years of experience in wireless phone market development."

And what a coincidence, the objective on the résumé you submit says:

Objective—to work for a Fortune 500 American-based telecommunications company where I can put to work my 10 years of experience in Argentina and Venezuela with Verizon and use my fluency in Spanish.

Do you think if I am the HR Manager working hard to fill that opening I am not going to read the rest of your résumé? It almost hit me over the head. Your job is to make HR's job easier. If you can match your résumé to the job why not do it?

When you write a synopsis of yourself that says, "hard driving sales manager, good work ethic…seeking a challenging job with a growing company…" all I see is "blah, blah, blah." If your résumé has an objective and It's anything like "I am looking for a challenging position with a growing company where I can use my management experience to advance my career," blow it up right now. This objective is all about you! HR doesn't care one bit what you want. It's all about who can they hire for the position that will make them look like a star.

EXPERIENCE

Ah, the crux of any résumé, the part every would-be employer scrutinizes to determine whether you can do the job.

Note past work experiences in terms of transferable skills that highlight how well you match the open position. Begin every descriptive phrase with an action verb, such as *managed, achieved, developed.*

Include key accomplishments and make them quantifiable. If your strength is sales, note that you "generated more than $1 million in sales," or exceeded your sales goal by 35% the first year. If you helped save your current employer money, say, "reduced overhead 15%." These particulars will impress and often encourage a would-be employer to think in terms of how you can help them achieve what you did for your previous company.

Even if you have been working for 40 years, you still need to keep your résumé to two pages. How do you possibly do that? One way is to summarize the first 20 years. For example, "1972-1990: Taught high school math and created an offsite tutoring program and raised a family." The other option is to highlight the relevant experience during the last 20 years and downplay the less relevant: "Taught high school math, 1972-1981."

 Action Verbs

As a rule, you want to avoid using verbs in letters or résumés that are placid and flabby, that don't create a sense of activity and movement. These are the types of "action verbs" you want to use:

Achieved	Administered	Advised	Analyzed	Appointed
Assessed	Audited	Centralized	Certified	Converted
Converted	Created	Designed	Determined	Developed
Directed	Documented	Employed	Enforced	Established
Evaluated	Executed	Expanded	Forecast	Formed
Formulated	Generated	Guided	Hired	Implemented
Improved	Increased	Initiated	Inspected	Instructed
Interpreted	Interviewed	Introduced	Investigated	Launched
Maintained	Managed	Minimized	Negotiated	Obtained
Operated	Organized	Planned	Presented	Processed
Produced	Published	Purchased	Recruited	Reduced
Referred	Regulated	Reorganized	Reported	Resolved
Resorted	Revitalized	Saved	Simplified	Sold
Solved	Staffed	Standardized	Studied	Supervised
Surveyed	Tested	Traded	Trained	Upgraded

EDUCATION

Unless this is your first job out of college do not list your grade point average. Besides your major, if you took courses that would be specifically beneficial to an employer, be sure to mention them. Note any honorary societies, academic honors or graduation distinctions, such as Dean's List, Cum Laude, Merit Scholar and sports or school clubs in which you excelled. Remember, you are trying to impress HR and set yourself apart.

Be sure to list any achievements like Eagle Scout—few people achieve it and it is very impressive at any age.

I recently saw a résumé in which the applicant cited a 2.2 (out of 4) grade point average *for his major*. Ouch! If your GPA is that low, don't advertise it. Your job is to minimize anything that might cause an employer pause. Never lie on a résumé. You will be found out and fired. If as an employer I can't trust you to be honest on your résumé, then when can I trust you? Highlight, accentuate or down play—yes: lie or mislead—never!

MILITARY BACKGROUND

If you've served in the armed forces, be sure to use that experience to your advantage. Employers hold the training that service members receive, even if it's not directly applicable to a specific job, in high regard. This is especially true in communities with a significant military history or presence. In a job search, we each use every advantage we have. If you are a veteran, ride the surge of patriotism as far as you can. You deserve it!

ACTIVITIES, ACCOMPLISHMENTS AND PERSONAL INTERESTS

This part of the résumé reveals a little bit about the real you, what you like to do when you're not at work, and let's a little of your personality come out. It helps show that you are a well-rounded person with compelling interests and activities—characteristics of a solid, stable, successful employee—and, someone I would like to work with!

You can really set yourself apart here, for good or bad, so be careful. Briefly outline your involvement in community organizations, such as Rotary Club, Habitat for Humanity or Girl Scouts. List hobbies and sports that interest you, with an emphasis on activities in which you excel as a leader. For example, if you coach a Little League team, mention it. It helps employers envision you as a leader.

It may be good to know that you were captain of the college tennis team. It's a little scary to know your hobby is knife throwing, which I saw on one résumé. Be interesting; don't appear weird or boorish.

If your interests are reading, watching old movies and knitting, don't list them. You sound like a couch potato who will put all your co-workers to sleep. I like to play racquetball, which not many people play anymore. There's an ongoing joke at our company that anybody whose résumé lists racquetball as a personal interest automatically gets an interview. The boss likes racquetball, this candidate plays racquetball so, ergo, they may like each other. That's not necessarily true or even likely, but they usually get an interview.

To recap, here are 10 quick tips for producing an effective résumé:

1. Keep it simple, honest and straightforward. Avoid gimmicks.
2. Keep it to two pages—max. (Unless certain fields like education require more.)
3. Emphasize your job accomplishments and results. Quantify your experience and achievements whenever possible. Sell yourself, but don't exaggerate.
4. Eliminate any unaccounted for gaps in time.
5. Avoid flashy artwork or images, unless, of course, you're an artist, model or in the arts. Do not use fancy fonts.
6. Use standard 8 ½ by 11-inch, high quality white paper.
7. Avoid complete paragraphs (be concise) and confusing abbreviations.
8. Use target keywords and bullets or asterisks for lists.
9. Do not cite personal references.
10. Carefully proofread for spelling and grammar, and then do it again. Remember, in a competitive job market, with many compelling applicants, employers will seize upon the smallest thing to help make their decisions easier. You don't want to yank yourself out of contention because you misspelled a word.

Scannable Résumés

Aside from small businesses, most companies now automate their résumé intake. They accept only résumés submitted online. It's an understandable limitation. Large companies often receive hundreds, even thousands, of résumés each day or week.

One way these companies handle the résumé deluge is to use keyword searches. Hiring managers employ programs that scan incoming résumés for specific words or phrases. They're looking for matches that will direct the résumé to the appropriate job opening. Using the earlier example of the job opening for a bilingual international sales manager in the telecommunications division in Latin America, HR will select four or five words deemed descriptive of that specific job: international, management, sales, telecommunications, and Latin America. As résumés come in, they are scanned for those keywords. If four or more pop up, that résumé will likely be directed to a human for review and follow-up. Thus, scannable résumés need to be easily "read" by computers to avoid being exiled to digital oblivion.

You see the importance of linking your job objective to relevant job descriptions. You need to anticipate what four or five keywords might be used to search résumés for jobs you're interested in, and make sure your résumé has them.

Here's an extra tip: It's appropriate to include extra keywords at the bottom of your résumé. I know it sounds strange and looks odd, but there's solid logic behind the practice. The term "call center" is widely used in the eastern half of the United States. In the west, the preferred phrase is "customer service center." In reality, they're the same thing and if you've worked for one, you want to make sure that recruiters in both halves of the country recognize your experience.

Many of the keys to a good traditional résumé apply to scannable versions as well, such as using compelling keyword nouns to describe your abilities and experience. Use language and acronyms that are specific to your industry, but avoid senseless jargon. Expand your keyword list with specifics, such as listing the names of software programs you use, including versions.

Résumé Structure

How you structure your résumé—that is, how you arrange the necessary blocks of information about yourself and your experiences—is mostly a matter of taste, though some formats are more effective at emphasizing certain strengths and minimizing weaknesses. Your first résumé-building decision is one of format: chronological, functional or a combination.

The *chronological résumé* is the most popular and widely accepted format. It is organized by job title and presents your work experience in reverse chronological order, with your current or last job cited first. Chronological résumés are easy to read and can quickly be reviewed by managers looking at employment histories. They want the freshest, most recent experience first and up front since that's generally considered the most important and relevant information. The more distant the job experience, the less important it becomes.

Use a chronological résumé when:

- Your job history is steady and consistent, with no major gaps in employment
- You haven't changed career tracks recently
- Your course of employment includes positions that display a progression of jobs with increased responsibility and scope
- Your past position titles are impressive and/or you were recently employed at a well-known company
- Your major career accomplishments were achieved in your most recent position

A *functional résumé* highlights your career skills, accomplishments and qualifications at the top of the document. It emphasizes your talents and abilities, what you can do more than where you've done it. Your employment history (e.g., experience) is not the focus. It is positioned lower in the résumé.

Use a functional résumé when:

- You want to emphasize your skills and accomplishments outside of your most recent position
- You've been out of the job market for an extended period of time
- You've held a variety of unrelated jobs
- You're switching careers

The *combination résumé* blends and amplifies the benefits of both chronological and functional résumés. It begins with a summary (functional format) of your most impressive qualifications, skills and accomplishments, followed by an employment history section highlighting your career experience and strengths.

Use a combination résumé when:

- Your employment history is steady and progressive
- You are applying for a position for which a chronological résumé is expected, but you also want to emphasize qualifications from earlier positions or from experiences outside of your career history
- You want a fast, effective way to match your skills to job requirements

THANK YOU NOTES

Sending a thank you note is more than mere courtesy. It's a way to extend the conversation, reinforce a message, set yourself apart from other job applicants and move the ball forward. There are no real secrets to an effective thank you note. Indeed, the basics are pretty straightforward:

- Do not send an email thank you note, which is used only when you care enough to send the very least. It lacks personality. (Twitter is even worse.) The practice suggests minimal effort. Heck, an emailed thank you note could be a form letter. Instead, use high-quality cards or personal stationery. Avoid anything that's ostentatious, gimmicky or humorous. You're not looking for a laugh. You're looking to make a good, professional impression. That means not using flowery, pink thank you notes that you might find lying around your house. Ideally, your correspondence should be monogrammed and personalized. If that's prohibitively expensive, there are abundant, tasteful choices at stationery stores.
- Personally write your note. If you have lousy handwriting, go slow. Take a moment. Practice your penmanship if you must. A note jotted in illegible hand is almost worse than not sending a note at all. If the recipient can't read what you write (or really has to work at it), what's the point? Remember, an employer will also be using your note as an example of your work. You send a sloppy note and I will assume you will send a sloppy note to my biggest customer. Not good.
- Be brief. It's a note, not a treatise.
- Be specific in your comments. Refer to actual elements of a conversation or meeting. Let the recipient know you were not just listening, but also thinking.
- And send thank you notes to everyone you interview with, not just HR. The fact that several people were either on a panel or met with you privately during the day means they will all have some input on the decision to hire you or someone else for the job.

I frequently get notes like this:

"Dear Mr. Blair, Thank you so much for the excellent seminar today. I liked your ideas. Thank you again, XXXX."

The note really says nothing except that the sender attended a seminar. I don't know what seminar he's talking about, let alone his notion of "great ideas." He could hardly be less memorable—except maybe that he says thank you a lot. Once is enough.

Deliver the note by hand the next day, if possible. That doesn't mean you have to stand outside a building and corner the intended recipient coming into work. You can leave the note with an assistant or colleague. A hand-delivery serves two purposes: One, it better ensures your note arrives at its destination in a timely manner and; two, it underscores your seriousness and determination. It also gives you a chance to get to know the receptionist or the boss' assistant a little bit, which is almost always a good thing. Going the extra step is usually noted.

If circumstances require you to mail your note, do so the same day as the interview, if possible, so that the recipient gets it the next day while you're still fresh in his or her mind. I suggest people address the envelope and put the stamp on it before the interview. Then you merely have to write the note and you are good to go. Drop the note off at a post office if that helps ensure it gets there faster.

In the course of a month, I receive lots of thank you notes. Over my career, I've probably received thousands. I open them all. To be honest, I often don't recall the sender (some of whom I may have met in large, group settings), but usually an effective thank you note from someone I've interviewed will achieve its intended purpose: It will jog back to mind its sender. I will recall who they are and what kind of job they were seeking. More importantly, the note will frequently oblige me. They've sent me a thank you note, which has reminded me I agreed to call John Smith on their behalf. In the rush of the day, I may have forgotten all about it, but you haven't.

Some examples of actual thank you notes, good, bad and ugh-ly:

Good

> Dear Phil,
> Thank you for providing great insider tips, suggestions and bubbly enthusiasm at the recent Job Search/Skill-Building seminar. You inspired me. Your idea about putting keywords on résumés was particularly enlightening. I appreciate the renewed spirit you bring to all of us "Career Managers" as we search for our next opportunity.
> Regards,
> XXXXXXX

Bad
> Dear Phil,
> Thanks for the meet. Interesting stuff.
> Best,
> XXXXXXX

Ugh-ly
> Dear Phil,
> I wanted to take this moment to express my appreciation for your time and advice last week. It was very good and I have taken it much to heart. I am sure it will help me moving forward.
> Love,
> XXXXXXX

The merits and demerits of the notes above should be pretty obvious. In the "good" note, the writer gets straight to the point, specifically mentions an event and something she learned and refers to a key philosophy: We must all proactively manage our careers. I know she paid attention and valued my time.

The "bad" note barely qualifies as a note. The language is too casual ("meet!"), too vague (no reference to when the actual meeting occurred) and insultingly bland. This person would have been better off not sending a note at all. Saying something is "interesting" is another way of saying you don't have anything to say. Avoid the word whenever possible

Finally, the "ugh-ly" note is also somewhat vague and wishy-washy. Where the note truly crashes is in the closing. I'm all for love, but a thank you note is not the same as writing lyrics for a song. Signing off "Love," is absolutely the wrong sentiment to evoke in what is essentially a business communication. It's inappropriate and, in this case, unsettling since the writer was a big, strapping fellow who I barely knew. The writer, of course, didn't really intend his ending to be taken literally and I did follow up to help him further with his job search. But his felicitous faux pas underscores a point I cannot make too often: Be careful with your words. Make sure they say what you mean and that you mean what you say.

The Value of Manners

Good manners are a kind of social lubricant. They help people and societies get along with each other. They create, foster and promote harmony. They are essential to our well-being, both as individuals and as a society of individuals.

This is true as well when you're seeking a job. Bad manners virtually guarantee a poor interview and failure. For guidance and advice on manners, there are lots of places to go: books, websites, newspaper columns. Here, though, are my top 10 tips in terms of job interviewing:

1. Be prompt. Better yet, be early—just not too early or you seem desperate.
2. Be courteous and polite to everyone you meet. A good impression at the front desk is important. Hold doors open, female or male. Say please and thank you.
3. Turn your cell phone off.
4. Greet people using their names.
5. Smile often and sincerely.
6. Make frequent eye contact.
7. Shake hands firmly.
8. Listen intently. Don't interrupt.
9. Answer succinctly.
10. Be perceptive. Stay in the moment. Survey your situation constantly and use your best judgment.

The All-Important References

At some point, if the interview process is moving along, you will be asked to provide references. References are very important and require smart management. Making the right choices are obviously critical to success. These are the people who will be asked to speak about you and for you. Choose them and manage them wisely.

Whether you are asked to provide one or five references, you want to strive for balance and diversity. You want to include current or recent co-workers, long-time professional contacts and colleagues, and ideally, supervisors who were sorry to see you go. These references should be people you know well—and who know you well. They should be able to speak knowledgeably about your professional and personal attributes. They should be individuals who respect you and desire your success. It is not appropriate to list family or friends as references. That's just silly and HR notices it.

If this is the first time you're compiling a list of references, or it's been a long time, here are some tips:

- If you haven't spoken to a prospective reference in a while, call, email or visit the person. You have to update them on your career search and demonstrate why you are worthy of their support.
- Provide your references with as many details as possible about your current job search. Give them a copy of your latest résumé. Include explanations about why you want this specific job and why you feel you are qualified for the job. Tell them why you want them to be a reference and be as specific as you can about what aspect of your working past you would like them to highlight. Do not list references on a résumé and do not say "references upon request." No need to state the obvious. Your reference list is to be prized and not abused. You don't want a possible employer contacting a reference before you've had a chance to brief them. Be sensitive about when and how often you turn to your references.
- Inform your references every time you supply their names and contact information to a potential employer. Ideally give them the name of the person who will be calling so they can be expecting the call, that way they will not be surprised when that employer calls. This will be a good time to go over any talking points—give them the job description and why you think you're the perfect candidate, clear up foggy names, dates or memories. If you have a weakness in a certain area, explain how you will compensate for it. You want your references to be your best salespeople. Ask them to contact you each time a potential employer contacts them. If an employer spends valuable time checking references that is a very good sign that they are seriously considering you for the position.

When your job search is complete (success!), send a letter, card or email to your references thanking them for their assistance and kind words. Who knows? You might need them again. And every reference is always curious to know whether you get the job or not.

QUESTIONS A REFERENCE MIGHT BE ASKED
Hiring managers call references to confirm details on an applicant's résumé and to clarify or flesh out points of interest or concern. It's a way of getting to know the person better, but from a third perspective.

Here are some typical questions that employers ask references, which you can use to help prepare your references:

- How would you describe the applicant's professional style?
- What was the applicant's most significant contribution to your organization?
- Why did the applicant leave your company?
- What are the applicant's strengths? Weaknesses?
- What type of management style best fits the applicant's personality?
- How would you describe the applicant's relationship with his or her work peers? With his or her supervisors?
- Given the described potential position at our organization, would you hire/rehire the applicant for the job? If not, why?

YOUR REFERENCE LIST

When you are asked to provide a list of references, you should do so in a manner akin to how you presented your résumé. The list should be printed on paper matching your résumé. It should be neat and clear, listing your name, phone number and email address at the top of the page in the same format and typeface as your résumé.

Next, include the following about each of your references: Make it as easy as possible for the HR Department:

- Full name
- Position or title
- Company name (and what the company does)
- Company address
- Office phone
- Home or cell phone (but only if the reference has explicitly given approval)
- Relationship to you (co-worker, supervisor, etc.)

Just when you think you have heard it all…Sally Luck, the HR Manager at KUSI, the TV station that airs my weekly employment segments, told me she asks interviewees who she is very serious about to bring three references with them when they interview. One time when she went out to the lobby to get the candidate, there were four people in the lobby. The candidate had literally brought his three references with him to the interview! We laughed so hard, I forgot to ask if she hired the person.

REFERENCE LETTERS AND GENDER

Other than applying to grad school, reference letters seem pretty passé. Employers typically prefer to speak directly with previous employers, rather than rely upon a written letter. But if a potential employer does ask you for a reference letter, beware, especially women.

If you think that a good reference letter for a man is a good reference letter for a woman too, you would be wrong. The qualities touted in recommendation letters for men differ sharply, and those differences can hurt a woman's chances at being hired.

A recent study out of Rice University (published in the Journal of Applied Psychology) reviewed 624 letters of recommendation for 194 applicants for eight junior faculty positions at an American university. The researchers discovered that letter writers generally conformed to traditional gender stereotypes and norms.

Female job candidates were typically described in social or emotive terms while male candidates were described in more active or assertive terms.

For example, adjectives used for female job seekers included sympathetic, tactful and agreeable. They were often described as taking direction well, helpful to others and able to maintain relationships.

Male job seekers, on the other hand, were described using adjectives like confident, ambitious, forceful, outspoken and intellectual. They spoke assertively, influenced others and initiated tasks.

The researchers then rated the strength of the letters and the likelihood the candidate would be hired based on a letter. They removed names and personal pronouns (thus disguising the gender of the applicant), controlled for variables like job experience and position sought, and asked faculty members to evaluate them.

Not surprisingly, reference letters written for men fared better than those for women. The men were more likely to be hired.

My point: Look hard at your letters of reference. If you're a woman seeking a job or promotion, compliments about your warmth and nurturing nature are nice, but would-be employers aren't looking for hugs. They're looking for motivated, self-directed, hard-working, focused, team-playing employees. Make sure your reference letters say as much, whether they are written *by* a male or female, or *about* a male or female.

If I am asked to write a reference letter and am willing to do it, I first tell the requester to have the person call me, that I prefer to talk to them. If the reference has to be in writing and again, I am willing to be a reference for this person, I tell the requestor to write the letter themselves. This way, they can emphasize the point they want and avoid me second-guessing them. I have them send the letter to me. I massage it into something I am comfortable with and then submit it. A winner all the way around: It saves me time and allows the job candidate to get their point across through me.

Presenting Your Credentials

By this point, you've done a lot of work. You should be proud, but not yet satisfied. That will come later. More serious tasks loom ahead. You know what the process is, résumé to references. Now we need to get you to the right position, at the right time, with the right person who can make you a job offer—that "You're Hired" moment.

Now is the time to present your credentials—so carefully compiled and crafted—to prospective employers. You'll notice I said "present your credentials," not "submit." *Submission*, as Dan Burns notes in his fine book, *The First 60 Seconds: Win the Job Interview Before it Begins*, implies merely sending something out, such as a résumé or cover letter. *Presentation* implies much more. It refers to a face-to-face meeting where real progress can be made.

Making first contact with prospective employers boils down to three principle objectives:

1. Getting your materials to the right person
2. Getting them noticed
3. Getting an interview

These can be challenging obstacles, but they are not insurmountable. Let's tackle them one by one.

Your first task, obviously, is to make sure the right person at your target company sees your application and supporting materials. Too often, I've found, job applicants send off résumés to general addresses, physical or electronic, with virtually no chance that someone with the ability to decide their fate will actually see them. It may feel good in the moment to mail off a bunch of résumés, but if you haven't ensured that it's going to go to the right, specific person, you've wasted effort and time. What you have found is "the big black hole."

I'm reminded of Marilyn, a woman who sent me a strong critique after listening to some of my advice on a TV segment. She said my suggestions for finding a job were, well, unprintable. Her proof was that she had sent out more than 2,000 résumés over the past year and she was still unemployed. Not one of the résumés elicited a response, let alone a job offer.

I don't know what her résumé looked like or the details of her job search, but judging from the anger of her critique, she was deeply frustrated and desperate. I think her anger and frustration must have come out somehow in her submissions.

Often there is no easy way to identify the right person to receive your résumé. Remember, your digitized application will likely pass through some sort of automated filtering, the keyword search we talked about earlier.

If there is an official application, read it carefully. Answer as precisely and specifically as possible. If the application requires descriptive writing or asks that you attach any sort of cover letter, use the right keywords so that your application will stand out.

There are advantages and disadvantages to filing an electronic application.

On the plus side, it tends to be faster and easier. The final result conforms to what companies want and expect. You can send your information to anyone, anywhere, anytime.

On the negative side, there's always a sense that you've shipped your information off into space (or cyberspace, in this case) with no assurance that it will arrive at its intended destination. Or that it will arrive anywhere.

To help make sure that doesn't happen to you, do some homework. If the job posting you're interested in lists a specific email address, great. If there's a specific recipient named, even better.

If not, the websites of most companies have links to their human resources department that may provide the appropriate information. If not or if you're in doubt, don't hesitate to call and ask. See if you can get the hiring manager's name, title and contact information. After you hang up, try it. Confirm that it's correct.

A tip: If you're directly emailing an individual, attach your presentation package, but cut and paste your cover letter into the body of the email. It's a great way to immediately establish who you are and the nature of the email. It greatly enhances the chances that HR will read it.

Less often these days, an actual person will conduct the initial filtering of applicants. The smaller the company, the more likely you will talk with a real person. All the more reason not to ignore small businesses when looking for work. Personal interaction is a good thing, providing you've done your homework and smartly crafted your presentation.

Confident Versus Cocky

An interview question that seems innocuous when asked is, "How did you hear about this job?" Simple enough question on the surface, but it could derail you. Be careful not to name-drop. If a reference is high up in the company, it can be the kiss of death to overemphasize your connection. It might be seen as arrogance or intimidation that you are trying to go over HR's head. A better way is to have the senior person get to HR before you do so you don't get that question. But if you do, come across as very grateful, not overly confident.

There are at least two possible answers to, "How did you hear about this job?" one of which is definitely better. You might respond, "Oh, I saw it on the website and submitted my résumé and here I am." You sure aren't coming across as having worked very hard to get the job and are way too complacent. HR wants to know you put some effort into getting where you are sitting now.

The better alternative is something like, "I heard about the opening when I was speaking with my uncle, Joe Smith, who works in the marketing department. He told me what a wonderful company XXX is and suggested I look into the position on the website. I did and followed up by dropping off my résumé with your assistant, Angie. What a nice lady she is! I discovered we share a love for traveling in South America."

The second answer is far more compelling. It incorporates a compliment for the company, mentions a relative working there who recommended the applicant for the job, and even extols the interviewer's assistant, who probably has some influence of her own. My point: Think about your responses to even the most innocent of questions and how you can turn any reply into a "why-you-should-hire-me" opportunity.

I was recently handed a résumé in a nice-looking folder that had the word "résumé" embossed on the cover. It was classy, not too pretentious. Obviously, I remember it. On the other hand, I can't recall the person who created it. Style is nice, but it's still all about substance, what's behind the cover. But this simple, inexpensive folder did get my attention, so think about it.

First-timers and Another-timers

What if you're returning to the workforce after many years away? Often, in the case of the latter, people quickly give up because they think their skills are obsolete or that they have nothing new to offer. The opposite is true.

If you're looking for your first full-time, career-oriented job out of college then you'll focus on describing talents applied elsewhere in your life. For example, your leadership skills if you were president of your school's student government, your organizational skills as a committee chairman of a club or fraternity, your diligence and doggedness as captain of the water polo team, your civic-mindedness as a reading tutor at a local elementary school. Again you will highlight how you developed leadership skills, showed initiative and made very good use of your spare time. And especially emphasize internships and volunteer work.

If you paid your own way through college, or even part of the expenses, be sure to mention that in your cover letter. If you worked while going to college, be sure to point that out, too. Both putting yourself through college and working while studying are very impressive to we HR people. Life was not handed to you on a silver platter. You showed initiative and perseverance, that you value education and did what you had to do to get your degree. We interpret that as you saw a valued target—a degree—and finished the project. Just the kind of people we want working for us.

If you started on your degree, no matter what the level, and didn't finish the degree, then you have some explaining to do. There may be good reasons but you better tell us how you are going to continue working on that goal until you reach it. Otherwise we interpret you as a quitter. Not the kind of people we want to hire.

If you are re-entering the job market after many years (perhaps you took time off to raise a family or tend to elderly parents), you can similarly draw upon any experiences you had during that time. Did you do charity work? If so, what skills were employed? Did you assist in your children's classrooms? Do you run a book club? Taking extension courses in a specific field of interest, getting an advanced certification, or a new degree are very impressive uses of your time.

Most of us have done something productive with our free time. If you haven't held a job for awhile, employers want to know how you've used that time, whether you used it well and to what end. If you took night classes, be sure to mention them, even if they relate more to a hobby than a job. At the very least, it shows you're engaged in life.

Employers know it is much harder to motivate and guide volunteers who are not being paid to do something. Exploit that fact. You need to be able to articulate that your success in helping put on the local school play or keeping the books at your church translate into skills and abilities an employer can appreciate and use. What skills did you learn while volunteering that will make you a better employee for my company and how do those skills apply to this specific job?

Dress for the Job You Want

Generally speaking, how you dress for a job interview won't get you the job, but it can easily jeopardize your chances. Clothes don't make the man or woman, but in the first moments of a first meeting with a hiring manager, they speak for you before you can speak for yourself. What they say may prove indelible. At the end of the interview cycle, when the interviewer is reviewing stacks of résumés and notes, you want the interviewer to remember what you said, not what you were wearing. Your clothing selection is a visual description of your taste and style. It's 100% you, good or bad. Like a résumé, phone call, cover letter or thank you note, your wardrobe is a tool. It should be used to enhance your overall presentation, to add subtle emphasis to desirable qualities like strong self-esteem, organization and responsibility. People who dress well generally look and feel confident and do well. Once you know the dress code at the company you are interviewing with show up for the interview one step dressier than expected. It's a sign of respect and visually you look like you belong at that company in a leadership role.

Have an outfit or two for those first few interviews. Remember, an interviewer at Company B doesn't know you wore the same suit to an interview at Company A.

So let's review the basics:

For women, conservative dress is essential. This is absolutely not the time to show cleavage or be provocative. You risk making the interviewer uncomfortable and it suggests poor judgment. I feel this way every day at the work place; cleavage is inappropriate and degrades women as professionals. I also think in these days of concern about sexual harassment, it sends the wrong message. I don't know what the male version of showing cleavage is but I hope you don't do it, whatever it is.

I tell cash-strapped college kids to take one dress shirt to the cleaners and have it professionally laundered, starched and pressed. Use that shirt for job interviews. As soon as the interview is over, take off the shirt, hang it up. You can get quite a few wearings out of your two-dollar investment at the cleaners. A young man I was interviewing once took this advice a bit too literally. He took the shirt off on the sidewalk outside of my office and carried it to his car. Remember we look out our windows and often see the real you in the parking lot after the interview. Drive away from the company in interview mode, it certainly can't hurt.

NECKWEAR

Choose a tie or scarf that smartly accentuates your outfit. Don't use an accessory to make a statement or start a conversation. You don't want to be remembered as the guy with the really strange tie.

SHOES

You can't go wrong with black, leather and polished. Make sure your shoes aren't at the end of their days. I think it was Aristotle Onassis who wisely said, "You can tell much about a man by the state of his fingernails and his shoes." Be conservative. That advice applies to women too: No stiletto heels.

Aristotle Onassis had two other gems of wisdom. If you can't eat dinner in the best restaurants then at least go there for a drink, just so you are seen in the best places, and if you have only one great outfit, just be sure to wear it with different people every time.

ACCESSORIES

Maximize with the minimum. Wear a wristwatch. It shows you value time. Don't wear an oversized, three-pound diver's watch or something with Mickey Mouse on the face. Wear minimal jewelry that is subtle and stylish.

Presumably, you'll be coming to your interview with a purse, briefcase or business portfolio, the latter two containing extra copies of your résumé and other materials you think might be useful or necessary. They should be business-appropriate. A daypack or some sort of goofy messenger bag is not.

Leave everything else in your car—including your cell phone. You won't need to call anyone during the interview.

If I'm doing an interview and dressed in a suit and tie, I expect the candidate to be similarly dressed. I've had young people come to meetings wearing T-shirts and jeans. By underdressing for our meeting, they're disrespecting me and the moment. If you don't know the dress code for an interview, call the company and ask. Or simply dress as nicely as you can. Nobody's going to mark you down for presenting yourself too well.

Dissecting Real Résumés

I gave you websites to go to for detailed résumé writing information. But I thought I would take one résumé that I received for deeper examination. The name is changed to protect the innocent. If he is still using this résumé, I doubt he is working. This is how HR would review a résumé.

JOHN SMITH
LOS ANGELES, CA 90001
Email: JSMITH@email.com
OBJECTIVE: CEO/PRESIDENT/EXECUTIVE DIRECTOR/PROGRAM MANAGEMENT

Executive Summary:

10+ years in executive management successfully controlled the P/L up to 13 billion USD; teamed up with collaborative incorporation who accurately successfully delivered the specification & requirement services for the international commercial and governmental sectors; et more...

Professional Performance:

Executive Director
MacrotimeProjex   San Francisco, CA   2005-Present
Provided records of successful delivery of the collaborative projects, whose face value's upto 60 million USD

Executive Director/Owner2
XYZ   San Francisco, CA   2000-2007
Partnered with the Owner1 to achieve the profit and revenue increased in the average of 35% yearly

Achieved Excellent Education

Master of Science in Management in Project Management
Wyoming Technical University   Meeteetse, WY 12/2005

Professional Development – Certified Awarded Certificate
University of California of Santa Cruz – Ext   Santa Cruz, CA 2/2004

Bachelor of Science in Applied and Computational Mathematics
Fresno State University   Fresno, CA 12/1999

WHAT'S WRONG WITH THIS RÉSUMÉ?

Where to begin?

Let's start with the résumé writer's information. It barely covers the basics, providing only a city of residence and an email address. Would-be employers almost always want and require more. What if a résumé reviewer really liked this particular applicant? Emails sometimes get to their destination late, or not at all. A phone number would be the quickest, more direct way to contact a job applicant—if they provide a number. If this person is waiting at home for his phone to ring, he's still waiting.

What's the applicant's job objective? Answer: President, chief executive officer, executive director or something in "program management." President of what?

The executive summary is supposed to provide that answer. But it is written so cryptically and poorly that it is almost information-free. We don't know what P/L is, only that it reached up to $13 billion in United States dollars. The résumé writer collaborated to deliver services to commercial and governmental sectors, but those services and their beneficiaries are not identified.

The actual writing and punctuation is terrible. Let's parse this phrase: "Teamed up with collaborative incorporation who accurately successfully delivered the specification and requirement services for the international commercial and governmental sectors; et more…"

"Teamed up with" and "collaborative" are redundant. "Accurately successfully" fails to accurately or successfully describe anything. Ending the summary with "et more…" is both grammatically incorrect and confusing. Why the ellipses? Is there more to come?

Even some of the spacing is wrong, the result of sloppy typing or copy editing.

The citations of past work experience and education are almost as bad as the executive summary. There is no clear indication of what the résumé writer did or does in these jobs. "Achieved Excellent Education" is clunky and, given the rest of the résumé, perhaps an exaggeration. I've read this résumé several times (way more than any real employer would) and I still have no idea what this job seeker wants or why he thinks he's qualified. I do know he has a "Certified Awarded Certificate," whatever that is.

15 Goofy Lines From Actual Résumés

We all have to keep our sense of humor⊠now more than ever. Here are some funny lines from actual résumés that someone collected. (Laugh, learn, do not repeat.)

1. "Although I am seeking an accounting job, the fact that I have no actual experience in accounting may seem discouraging. However..."
2. "Excellent memory; strong math aptitude; excellent memory; effective management skills; and very good at math."
3. "Extensive background in public accounting. I can also stand on my head!"
4. "Graduated in the top 66% of my class."
5. "I am a pit bull when it comes to analysis."
6. "I am relatively intelligent, obedient and as loyal as a puppy."
7. "I am the bestest person alive for this job, and you can't see that, it's your loss."
8. "I have a bachelorette degree in computers."
9. "I'll starve without a job but don't feel you have to give me one."
10. "I saw your ad on the information highway, and I came to a screeching halt."
11. "It's best for employers that I not work with people."
12. "My fortune cookie said, 'Your next interview will result in a job'— and I like your company in particular."
13. "My intensity and focus are at inordinately high levels, and my ability to complete projects on time is unspeakable."
14. "Note: Keep this résumé on top of the stack. Use all the others to heat your house."
15. "You have to give me the job, or my mother will be highly upset at you."

phil•osophy 101   **6**

When you get called in for a job interview, you deserve a pat on the back. Just getting the interview means you've successfully overcome significant hurdles to reach the BIG moment: Now let's make sure you shine!

Job seekers make the common assumption that an interview is an opportunity for the employer to grill the applicant, try to catch them off guard with trick questions or ask subliminal questions intended to probe their inner soul. The candidate présumés that since the interviewer called the meeting, the candidate has to sit there, "take it" and hopefully survive the inquisition.

Not true.

I want you to take control of every interview as if you called the meeting.

Think of it this way. You've worked really hard to get this interview. You've crafted a world-class résumé. You've networked like crazy. You've followed up on leads until your own mother thinks you're a pest. Now, the big job interview arrives and you, and most others, think you should take all the cues from the interviewer. It's their office. They called you, set the meeting time. They have the job you want.

That makes perfect sense, but I want you to think about the interview from a different perspective. Think of it from the interviewer's perspective: "I need to fill this position. My superiors are judging me on how fast I find the right candidate to hire. I want the person I am interviewing to come in here and sell me on why they are the best person for this job. Don't make me pull it out of you. Hit me over the head. Wow me with your talents and experience and how they apply to this exact position. Show me you are someone I would enjoy working with, that you understand the culture of our company, and most of all that you want the job!"

If you ever walk out of an interview thinking "I never got to mention my experience at ABC, or how my volunteer work at the YWCA was pertinent to the job," or anything else that would have shown you are a better candidate for the job, then shame on you. Don't come out of an interview with, "But she never asked me about..." I want you to walk out of the meeting thinking, "Dang, I made all my points, I hit on all cylinders, and if they don't select me, there was nothing else I could have done.

This is true whether you have a professional HR person conducting the interview (they will appreciate your initiative) or a small business owner or department supervisor who is perhaps less prepared and more nervous than you. Unless you're ready to seize the day, the interview will be a disaster, with failed expectations on both sides of the desk.

Regardless of how experienced or deft a job interviewer is, it's important—maybe critically so—for you to take charge of the meeting, but make sure you do it in a nice, polite, respectful way. Walk into the room and begin the conversation with pleasantries, how nice it is to meet the interviewer, what a beautiful view they have from their office, how excited you are to discuss the open position.

When the interviewer asks you, in one form or another, "Tell me about yourself," I want you to hear, "Why should I hire you? Why are you the perfect candidate and not the other ones?"

Think of an interview as the ultimate sales presentation, and you are the product you are selling. This is your moment. It is time to sell yourself, your experience, your education, your qualifications. Dig deep into the responsibilities of the job, and more than anything else, reach out and grab the job by making it clear that you're absolutely the best possible candidate. You want to be proactive, engaging, dynamic, self-assured and deeply interested in the job.

Yes, you need to pace yourself. The interviewer needs to think they are in control. They probably think they should lead the interview since in their mind they invited you to the meeting. Let them think they are guiding the meeting and be respectful. I want you to be able to highlight your strengths and make sure you get your points across. Hear and react to what the interviewer asks you, showing that you are a good listener, but make sure you ask questions as well. You know what aspects about you the interviewer needs to know. Make sure you weave them throughout the conversation.

And at the end of the perfect interview, you want the interviewer to think there is no other candidate for the job. You want to set the bar so impossibly high that potential employers think they'd be fools not to hire you. And, of course, they would be.

6

Interviewing

"It's okay to fail, but never okay to give up.**"**
—ANONYMOUS

"During job interviews, when they ask, 'What is your worst quality,'
I always say, 'Flatulence.' That way I get my own office.**"**
—DAN THOMPSON

"So many people out there have no idea what they want to do for
a living, but they think that by going on job interviews they'll magically
figure it out. If you're not sure, that message comes out loud and
clear in the interview.**"**
—TODD BERMONT

Nobody Likes Interviewing

The late, great actress Katherine Hepburn once opined that death would
be a great relief.

Why?

"No more interviews," she replied.

Hepburn, of course, was referring to the agony and tedium of being
endlessly queried as a movie star and celebrity. Still, most of us can relate—
at least a little bit. We tend to feel the same way about job interviews.

It may come as a surprise to some that human relations employees
often dislike conducting interviews almost as much as job candidates.
Imagine spending entire days speaking with tense job candidates, trying to
be warm and witty, open and friendly, while at the same time probing for
information or clues the candidate may not be willing to provide. It can feel
a bit like an inquisition—on both sides—but until someone comes up with
a better way of doing things, this is HR's best and only option.

An interview of some type is necessary for every job before someone can be hired. This is where the pedal hits the metal. It's the only direct way for employers to assess job candidates, up close and personal. Do they truly live up to the reputation and image presented in their cover letter, résumé and references? How do they handle themselves? What do they look like? Are they likeable in person? Would I want to work with them? Would I want to have lunch with them? Are they right for the job?

That's why job interviews are so dreaded. There's a lot riding on what happens during a job interview—a career can be made or sunk, depending on the outcome. Candidates all tend to sweat bullets, some literally when they are interviewed. Mostly because they don't feel prepared and have no idea what is going to be thrown at them.

Of course, there are a few nifty tricks to faring well in a job interview and I'll cover some of them with you in this chapter, along with a few caveats and cautionary tales. But more importantly, I'll show you how to prepare so that you know generally what to expect in any interview—and how to have the right responses firmly in mind. Maybe you'll even be comfortable and enjoy the experience.

Job interviews come in many shapes and sizes. I'm going to focus on the two most important types: the informational interview and the job interview. Let's start with the informational interview, which necessarily comes first, often long before a job interview. Do the first well and the second follows much more easily.

Informational Interviews

Throughout this book, I have talked about the value of networking—the process that never ends, even when you have the perfect job. The informational interview is the fundamental core of networking. Simply put, it means sitting down with someone to discuss one of three things: Your interest in that person's company, their industry or their own career path.

You may or may not know this person. Effective use of networking will get you in front of lots of people you don't know, but who you think can help you learn more about those three key categories. We're talking here about seeking "career option advice," which sounds a lot less desperate than "help me find a job." You are meeting with people as equals, discussing each other's past, current and future jobs. Typical topics are about how the industry is going, why they chose their career path and about the company they work for. Remember, you are not interviewing for a job, but if the possibility pops up—jump on it. You may have suggestions for them from your experiences. It is very appropriate to wind up the discussion asking who else in the company, or the industry, do they think you should speak with. It's "who do you know that they know" in its best form.

I like concluding an informational interview with job seekers asking, "Is there anything I can do for you?" Recently, I saw that the person I was meeting with had worked for a company that Manpower really wanted to turn into a customer, but had so far failed. I mentioned this and he replied that someone in Purchasing was a good friend. Within 24 hours, he had set up a meeting for our salesperson. The meeting was beneficial for both of us.

These referrals are the quickest, least threatening way to get in front of a potential decision maker at their company or another company. The person you are meeting with for an informational interview probably is not hiring at the time you talk with him or her. However he or she can still make a huge difference in your career search and ultimate success.

Some people balk at this notion. They ask why they should waste their time meeting with people who have no jobs to offer and may not influence the hiring decisions where they work. That's a bad presumption. Here's why:

First and foremost, anyone and everyone can make a difference in your job search. You might not know who will be instrumental, how or when, but you can be sure that sitting in front of a computer perusing classifieds and employment boards will never get you where you want to be. You want to be in front of people, discussing your career interests and gathering information, advice, leads and actionable tips from them. You are asking for a chunk of their time to learn from them about their industry, their company and/or their own career.

There's an amusing line I sometimes hear quoted by businessmen: "I know that half of all my advertising dollars are a waste. I just don't know which half until I spend them."

The same holds true for informational interviews. Probably half—if not more—of informational interviews are in fact a waste of your time, and the time of the person who has graciously agreed to meet with you. Which informational interview will help and which will not? Like the businessman's trenchant quote, it's an enduring conundrum. You don't know the answer, so let's learn and prepare together.

When someone asks for five minutes of my time I snicker inside. Nothing happens in any meeting that is five minutes long. How naïve do they think I am? I am often tempted to say yes to the "five minutes," confirm the five minutes and then hold them to it when they arrive. Bet they would never use that five minutes phrase again!

A more reasonable time to request is 30 minutes. It's not asking for a lot of time but some very meaningful dialogue can happen in half an hour. So why not ask for it upfront? If the meeting seems to be going well, meaning they are enjoying the conversation, learning from it or feeling like they are being helpful, they may be comfortable extending the time.

I am always impressed when someone I am meeting with stops the conversation to acknowledge our time is up, and ask if it is alright to continue. If they ask, I usually give them more time. If they don't ask then they are assuming they can stay as long as they would like and I find that disrespectful. They asked for the meeting, they should manage the time.

Preparation

Everything starts with preparation. Over the years, I've often been asked, "What is the number one mistake most job seekers make when they meet with you for an informational interview?" My answer is quick and easy: "IT'S LACK OF PREPARATION!"

Here is a typical scenario. It should give you some insight not just into what you need to do and say in an interview, but also what's going through the mind of the HR person.

I limit myself to one informational interview per day, otherwise it would be a full-time job. The person, whom I typically don't know, is looking for advice and guidance on finding a job, a little more direct than "career option advice." Since our company does nothing but put people in jobs, I am a great candidate with whom to meet. My assistant now has them go to the Job-Won.com website and download and read *Strategies for Success,* which outlines the basics of the job search. She does this because she wants them to have a fair chance with me, and being prepared is the most important piece of the puzzle.

Now keep in mind that getting an informational interview is an accomplishment in itself. Remember how I mentioned that at least 50% of informational interviews are likely to be a waste of your time. The percentage is a whole lot higher for the interviewer. That's an important point to bear in mind. The interviewer is committing time in their busy day to participate in what will likely be, from their point of view, a non-productive use of time. It is incumbent upon you to try to make it as productive a meeting as possible.

As I said, someone like me would be the ultimate informational interview. We specialize in hiring people, we work with HR representatives of major companies and small businesses throughout the community, and we hear about job openings long before they are posted. You don't want to blow such an opportunity. If someone uses a chit, or pulls a string to get an informational interview with me, they should be prepared for both their presentation to me and for my honest feedback. I do not balk at telling someone what they did wrong or need to do better. On the plus side, my observations are meant as friendly advice intended to help someone avoid the same mistake during a real job interview.

Roger, the son of a good friend who had just graduated from college, was having a devil of a time finding a job. My assistant escorted him in to my office and I did a double take—he was chewing gum. I asked him about it and he was very embarrassed and quickly said he had meant to "spit it out," (interesting choice of words in an interview) but had forgotten. As we talked more, I stopped him mid-sentence and asked him if he realized how many times he had cracked his knuckles in the short time we had been meeting. Right as he was saying he doesn't crack his knuckles, unconsciously he cracked them. Now he was embarrassed a second time. I sternly told him if he had been an applicant for a job with my company, I would have thrown him out the second I realized he was chewing gum. Likewise he would have been escorted out because of an unconscious irritating habit of cracking his knuckles.

Better he learn the error of his ways with me, a neutral observer, than to screw up an interview for the job of his dreams. I never knew what happened to that kid because, surprise, I never heard from him again. If you have nervous tics, get them under control before the interview. No matter what your education, experience or skill, they will most likely kill your job opportunity. The only exception I can think of are engineers who have very specific, hard-to-find skills.

Just like in a job interview, the job seeker should take immediate charge of the informational interview. After all, they asked for the meeting, so they should assume control of it.

Usually, the conversation begins with pleasantries like "Thanks so much for taking the time to meet with me. Jane has told me so much about you and Manpower." Blah, blah, blah. We've all heard and said such things. They're conversational lubricant, necessary to get things going and should be quickly followed by an explanation of why the person has asked to meet me, what they want to talk about and how I can help.

All too often, however, I've found job seekers to be alarmingly reticent, as if I'm supposed to know what we're going to talk about or the goals for the meeting. A rough beginning can be a case of nerves or uncertainty on the part of the job seeker, both completely natural and understandable, but it's still not acceptable. Now is not the time to appear confused and flustered; now is the time to be confident and forceful (in a nice way). You know why you're there. Let the other person (me) know too.

When a job seeker doesn't grab initial hold of a meeting, after an awkward silence, I tend to take charge. And I usually start with the same question: "What can I do for you?"

When I meet with someone as a favor, I don't want to intimidate them or put them on the spot. On the other hand, I don't go out of my way to make them feel comfortable and at home. This is an opportunity for them to rehearse their interview skills, not learn them. It's like a two-person play. I know my lines. I expect the other actor to know theirs.

I always seat the other person across from my desk. And yes, I have a large, "I-am-the-boss" kind of desk. It's actually a piece of art, lovely to look at, but it also serves a couple of important functions in meetings like this. It is a physical barrier between me and the job seeker, a visual power play that establishes the hierarchy in the room. I also have a couch and chairs in my office. They're nearby and quite comfortable. But during informational interviews (not to mention actual job interviews), they are strictly off-limits.

The reasoning should be obvious: I want visitors to experience a typical informational job interview. I won't be too tough or too easy. If I am either, it's not a true interview scenario and they can't do their best to impress me. I expect job seekers to be a little nervous, but not shaking in their boots. If they are, it means they're not really ready to conduct a successful informational interview, let alone a make-or-break job interview.

Once we're seated and pleasantries have been exchanged is the time to for you to kick off the conversation with why you actually asked for the informational interview. Remember the three reasons are:

- To learn more about his/her career path (CFO, Sales, etc.)
- To learn more about his/her industry (telecommunications, manufacturing, etc.)
- To learn more about their employer (Qualcomm, Nokia, etc.)

Always remember: You requested the informational interview. Much like dating, if you asked for the date, you are the de facto host. You take control of starting the conversation and interview them about one or more of the three reasons above. This is your chance to wow them with your knowledge because you have done your homework and prepared for this meeting.

The Job Interview

There are three primary steps to preparing for and doing well in an interview.

1. Fully understand your career history and professional strengths. You should be able to tell your story forwards and backwards, ably and persuasively. If you cannot, no one else can.

2. Practice your job interview skills until you've mastered them, until they become second nature. Study the interview do's and don'ts that I describe throughout this chapter. Remain calm and confident throughout your interview. It's not as if you're being stood up before a firing squad. If you've followed the advice of earlier chapters, done your homework and practiced, go in smiling. You'll knock them dead.

3. Develop CAR stories—short for Challenges, Actions and Results. These are brief narratives in which you are the star. Relate an experience to an interviewer in which you confronted a challenge, took action and got results. You should have several of them, each reflecting a different sort of accomplishment. CAR stories enhance the interview process and can be hugely helpful with open-ended questions that require you to illustrate your strengths and abilities. The open-ended questions used by an interviewer usually begin with, "Tell me about a time when..." These are called "behavioral interview" questions and are all the rage right now.

An example of a behavioral interviewing question might be, "Tell me about a time when you were not meeting a goal and what you did about it." Using the CAR approach detailed below, the abbreviated version of your answer would be: "Last year, we were 30% behind on our sales goal six months into the year. I sent all our sales staff to a sales training seminar for one week and, due to new sales techniques and re-energized motivation, within four months we were exceeding our sales goals."

How to Build a CAR

CAR stories can be surprisingly effective. They make a strong, positive impression upon employers because they illustrate specific Challenges, Actions and Results that you met, took and achieved.

Employers often ask leading questions designed to assess whether you fit their company's culture and plans. CAR stories are an effective way to turn a simple question into one that helps answer those concerns.

Just as we are all individuals with unique work histories and experiences, so too are our CAR stories. However, here are a series of questions you can ask yourself as you construct and then tune your CAR story.

C: Challenges you faced or encountered
- What needed to be accomplished to overcome the challenge?
- How and why did the obstacle arise and how did you discover it?
- How did you initiate action to remedy the situation?
- What were your specific assignments, responsibilities or duties related to carrying out the solution?

A: Actions you took to resolve the problem or situation
- What skills did you use (interpersonal, technological, multitasking, etc.) to achieve a solution?
- What was your solution and how was it successful?
- How did you execute your goals, plans and procedures?
- How were your actions creative or innovative?
- What did members of your team achieve under your supervision and guidance?

R: Results achieved
- What did you accomplish?
- Who benefitted and how?
- Can you quantify or measure the results?

The Actual Job interview

As I mentioned earlier, much of what you learn and perfect to conduct a successful informational interview applies naturally and directly to conducting a successful job interview. Remember the informational interview is much more data-gathering and does not involve a job opening. A job interview is directly related to a specific job opening. That shouldn't be surprising. If you learn to present an impressive case for yourself during an informational interview, you certainly can do so during the real thing.

By now, you should know a lot about what goes into a successful interview. You know how to dress and speak. You know what you're looking for in a job and career. You know yourself.

At its most fundamental, a job interview is all about questions—theirs and yours. It's the whole point of the meeting, after all. What makes it so harrowing is what Donald Rumsfeld, the two-time U.S. Secretary of Defense, once famously—albeit confusingly—referred to as the knowns and the unknowns:

"There are known knowns. These are things we know that we know. There are known unknowns. That is to say, there are things that we know we don't know. But there are also unknown unknowns. There are things we don't know we don't know."

Rumsfeld wasn't talking about job interviews, of course. To be honest, I don't know exactly what he was talking about—a case of a known unknown, I guess. But Rumsfeld's point seems to neatly apply to job interviews. To wit: Applicants go into job interviews knowing they will be questioned. They know—or think they know—what some of the questions will be. They also know they will be asked questions they cannot know in advance or anticipate.

Much of the rest of this chapter deals with questions. In some cases, I'll talk about possible responses, but mostly it will be up to you to come up with answers.

Generally speaking, interviewers ask three kinds of questions: positive, neutral and negative. You have to be prepared to capably and seamlessly respond to all three—often in the same interview. Here are some basic examples:

POSITIVE:

What are your strengths?
Why should we hire you?
What can you contribute to our organization?
Why do you feel you are qualified for this position?
How have you been successful in your career and why?
Tell me about job responsibilities you enjoy.
Describe your ideal job.
Tell me about a situation when you felt very effective in your job.

NEUTRAL:

What will your references, including former supervisors and co-workers, say about you?
How would you describe your communication style with supervisors, peers and assistants?

How do you handle working under pressure?
What are your salary requirements and expectations?
Why are you interested in this position?
What is important for me to know about you?
What are the key lessons you have learned in your career?
How do you set priorities?
How do you feel about relocation?

NEGATIVE:
Tell me about a work situation when you felt ineffective?
What did you not like about your last position, supervisor or company?
What is the biggest mistake you've made in your career?
Tell me how you've handled a difficult co-worker, supervisor or junior peer?
What have supervisors criticized about your work style?
What type of business environment do you find most challenging?

Before you go into any interview, review these questions and have answers in mind. More specifically, imagine questions the HR person is likely to ask about the particular job you're seeking or about your particular situation. Take time to work through your answers. Write them down. Rehearse them, if necessary. In the interview, you don't want to sound like your reading from a script, but you do want to know the answers well enough to deliver a response directly and without effort.

A job interview isn't just an opportunity for a potential employer to learn more about a job candidate. It's also an opportunity for the candidate to learn more about the employer, a company's philosophy, the different aspects of the job you're applying for and what the company requires of its employees. In other words, the questions you ask are as important to you as the questions asked of you. HR professionals really do want the interview to be a two-way discussion.

On a different note: I don't want you to walk out of an interview thinking, "What just happened here?" You chatted with the interviewer for two hours and know nothing more about the job than you did going in. In fact, you and the interviewer didn't have a professional conversation about the position, the company or the industry. This is most common with department managers who are not trained well by HR to conduct interviews for their departments. They usually are not professional HR staff, but rather company employees who may be conducting the interview because the open position falls in their department or they're familiar with the job. That might sound like sufficient qualification—and sometimes it is—but often you wind up with a person who senses the right job candidate boils down to, "Do I like this person?"

If you are serious about wanting the job, even when facing a potentially flaky interviewer, then you need to take control, just as we discussed in the introduction to this chapter. I really think the interviewer will thank you later.

When you step into a room for an interview, the person on the other side of the desk isn't always experienced—or even very good at what they do. Perhaps the most common example of this is what I call a "Chatty Cathy." Beware. Such people tend to talk about anything and everything, most of which has nothing to do with the actual job or its requirements. They'll pontificate about the weather or local sports team. They'll ask you personal questions that may actually be inappropriate and perhaps illegal. It's often a result of their being very nervous. So what do you do?

Take charge of the meeting. Subtly and gracefully, bring the conversation back to discussing the job, your excitement about it and the interviewer's expectations. If they persistently wander off topic, persist in equal measure.

At the end of the meeting, you want to have achieved two things:

1) Fully described why you're the right person for the job.
2) Done it in such a delightful way that the interviewer thinks he or she has just conducted the perfect interview.

You should have several questions already in mind going into the interview and an expectation that others might arise during the interview itself. Don't be afraid to write your questions down and bring them with you. Doing so will help you remember them, articulate them during the interview and improve your performance. Be sure to ask your questions respectfully, and from an informed perspective. You don't want to ask: "So does ACME have a good future?" Your questions should expand upon what you already know about the company from your earlier research.

Years ago I was hiring additional salespeople and a sharp, young articulate lady came in for an interview. We started talking about Manpower and she stopped me and said, "By the way, what does Manpower do?" I was flabbergasted. A salesperson of all people coming to an interview with zero knowledge of the company she was interviewing to sell for. After that comment, I can assure you it was a very short interview.

Here are some sample questions, which you can tweak to meet your particular circumstances:

ABOUT THE COMPANY
What future plans does the company have for this position?
What are some of the company's short- and long-term goals?
What is the company's corporate culture like? What are the company's values?
I am fascinated by the ABC new product. Can you tell me more about it?

ABOUT THE JOB
Is this a new or existing position? (If new, why was it created?)
With the areas of responsibility, what are the two or three most significant goals you would expect me to accomplish?
Where does this position fit within the company's structure?
What level is this position (entry, advanced, supervisory, etc.)?
What are the position's main responsibilities?
Who would I interact with in this position?
Which job duties/activities would I split my time between and how?
Are there opportunities for growth and advancement? If so, what additional career opportunities might be open to me?
What are the goals for the department I would work with?
How do they support the company's overall mission/goals?
What are the major challenges in this position (and for this organization)?

I suggest you take notes during the interview. And yes, it is very appropriate. A lot of issues may be discussed that you will want to remember later, maybe even to include in your thank you note and for polite follow-up collateral. Your notes might include such things as objectives of the department, key functions of the job and potential growth opportunities. Also, we, including HR folks, are impressed when someone feels what we said was important enough to write it down. You may be making your grocery list for your stop on the way home, but I don't know that.

Answering questions in an interview is as much about how you say it as it is about what you say. No answer should be shorter than fifteen seconds or longer than two minutes. Too short and it seems abrupt and rude. "Have you ever had bottom line responsibility?" If your answer is "No." it catches me off guard because I am not ready with the next question and it appears to me that you are dismissing my inquiry as unimportant to you. Instead, you might answer, "I have not had actual bottom line responsibility, but in our department at ABC company, we were all very aware of sales and costs of products and the manager reviewed the monthly P&L with the entire office. I am very aware of the importance of cost controls and hitting sales goals." Wow: a whole lot better than "No."

In your longer answer, you reinforced your knowledge, awareness and appreciation of the importance of hitting goals, especially sales and controlling costs. Without me asking directly, you just hit two of the hot buttons of every manager. High five to you!

Conversely, I don't want you to be a Chatty Cathy. Anything longer than two minutes and I have lost interest in whatever you are saying—and may even have forgotten what the question. I will spare you an example, but a rambling unfocused answer to my question is not the way to impress me. We all have a tendency to ramble when we get nervous—and an interview is clearly a nerve-wracking situation—but with practice and a timer you will become aware of how long you are speaking and get it under control.

If you feel it's an involved question that deserves extra time and detail, I suggest a "check-in," as in, "Am I going into too much detail? Am I answering your question? Would you like me to continue?" These are appropriate check-in questions. You may get a pleasant, "Oh no, please continue, this is very helpful and interesting." Or you may get a "Thank you, I've heard enough." If you get the latter, thank heavens you did a check in. If you get the former, you know you are hitting the bull's-eye!

Interviews From Hell

As serious as interviewing for a job can be, we also have to keep our sense of humor.

The Internet can be fantastically useful—and amusing. Vice presidents and personnel directors from 100 of the nation's largest corporations were asked to recount their most unusual experiences interviewing prospective employees. I can't really vouch for the absolute authenticity of their comments, but after decades of doing interviews, I can believe anything. Needless to say, I don't recommend any of the following:

- A job applicant challenged the interviewer to arm wrestle.
- The interviewee wore a Walkman, explaining that she could listen to the interviewer and music at the same time.
- The candidate fell and broke an arm during the interview.
- The candidate announced she hadn't eaten lunch and proceeded to eat a hamburger and French fries in the interviewer's office.
- The candidate explained that her long-term goal was to replace the interviewer.
- The candidate said he never finished high school because he was kidnapped and kept in a closet in Mexico.
- The balding candidate excused himself during the interview and returned a few minutes later wearing a toupee.
- The applicant said that if he were hired, he would demonstrate his loyalty by having the corporate logo tattooed on his forearm.
- The applicant interrupted the interview to phone her therapist for advice on how to answer specific interview questions.
- The candidate brought a large dog to the interview.
- The applicant refused to sit down, insisting on being interviewed while standing.
- The candidate dozed off during the interview.

Don't Talk the Talk

Cell phones are one of life's great conveniences. A casual glance around in almost any public situation is likely to reveal people talking/texting/reading/watching their mobile smartphone. Most of us can no longer leave home without one.

Just don't bring it to job interviews. Here's a true tale from a friend and associate named John, a senior vice president for human relations with a high-tech manufacturing firm, about a job candidate who didn't get the message:

Sam was an applicant for a senior engineering job and had gotten far enough in the process to merit a meeting with John. When he arrived for the meeting, John immediately noticed that Sam had a Bluetooth wireless headset stuck in his ear. John thought this a bit off-putting, but chose not to mention it. The candidate was, after all, an engineer.

The two men soon launched into a productive, interactive discussion, with John keeping the focus on the candidate's engineering talents and experiences. Suddenly, Sam's expression changes without obvious explanation. He touches his ear. His eyes dart back and forth. He becomes stony-faced, then completely quiet and still, almost as if under a sudden, unseen spell.

After a few silent, awkward moments with John just staring at him, the candidate whispers very quietly, "I'll call you back."

The candidate took a phone call in the middle of the job interview! This is wrong on so many levels that it's laughable.

First and foremost, the candidate should have turned his phone off before entering the interview. Surely, he could afford to be *incommunicado* for a relatively brief period of time that might substantially determine the future of his career.

Second, if you prefer to wear a wireless receiver like a Bluetooth, make sure you remove it before any interview. It should be standard practice to review your physical impression before any meeting. Check yourself out in a bathroom mirror. Or the rearview mirror of your car, if there's nothing else available. You don't want spinach stuck to your teeth. You don't want an LED-flashing bit of plastic hanging from your ear. Both are equally distracting to people you want entirely focused on why you're the person for the job.

Third, if you find that you've inadvertently kept your cell phone turned on and it rings, don't answer it. That's the natural reaction, of course, but doing so will likely kill any chance you have at the job you're seeking. Instead, apologize for the interruption and quickly switch it off. Everybody makes mistakes in the interview process. Interviewers know that. It's how people handle those mistakes that are most important.

In this case, the damage to the candidate's chances at the job was "cell-inflicted." In fact, John quickly ended the interview. Another guy got the job.

In his excellent book *201 Best Questions to Ask on Your Interview*, author John Kador offers 15 rules for framing and asking effective questions.

1. Ask open-ended questions that can't be answered with a "yes" or "no."
2. Keep the question brief.
3. Don't interrupt the answer.
4. Construct questions so that the answers emphasize the positive.
5. Use inclusive language, like "we" instead of "you."
6. Ask questions the interviewer can answer.
7. Avoid questions you can easily find the answer to.
8. Avoid "why" questions.
9. Avoid questions calling for a superlative, such as "What's the absolute best thing about this company?"
10. Avoid leading or loaded questions, such as "Don't you think employees who go above and beyond should get bonuses?"
11. Avoid questions that might be construed as threatening.
12. Avoid questions that sound desperate.
13. Avoid "what about me" questions. Frame them in terms of what you can do for the company.
14. Don't ask irrelevant questions.
15. Go ahead and ask the person if you're right for the job.

There are, of course, questions you shouldn't ask. Avoid asking your interviewer personal questions about their job experience, except as it may directly relate to the conversation. Such questions include asking how they got their job or what their opinion is of their company. These might seem important to you, but a first interview is not the time to ask them. It is also inappropriate during a first interview to directly inquire about salary, retirement plans, vacations, bonuses and holidays. It sounds very presumptive and cocky. These are subjects to be discussed when you are negotiating a job offer or have received one.

There are some questions you should never ask. Do not discuss personal topics or subjects like politics and religion. These are employment minefields that are bound to blow up in your face. You're walking blind here. You don't know your interviewer well enough to venture into these areas and, even if you think you do, a job interview is not the forum for such discussions.

Don't ask your interviewer's opinion of a former employee, for example, the person that had the job for which you are interviewing. It's inappropriate for the interviewer to talk about this kind of personnel matter and it's really none of your business. Stay focused on why you're there and why you're the right person for the job.

Thought-Provoking Questions

In the course of most interviews (especially those for serious and much coveted jobs), a tough or tricky question will come up, probably several in fact. The interviewer's intent isn't malicious. He genuinely wants to hear your answer. He also, if he is doing his job right, wants to see how you think on your feet.

He has two reasons. First, he wants to see if you have expertise in the area in which you are applying for work. You should be able to discuss in-depth topics about this field. Second, if you are hired, you may very well be standing in front of your company's largest customer someday. If he asks you an off-the-wall question, the HR interviewer wants some idea of how you will handle yourself.

Below are some sample questions and recommended responses. Before you get into an interview situation, ask yourself these questions, devise your answers and then practice them until they can be delivered quickly and smoothly, as if you never practiced at all.

1. Tell me a little about yourself. Don't begin with, "Well, I was born in a little town called..." The inquiry isn't personal. The interviewer really has no interest in your personal life and accomplishments—at least not right now. Talk about your career experience, achievements and qualifications.

I tell candidates when they hear this question what I think the interviewer is really asking is "Why should I hire you?" The interviewer thinks they are asking in a clever way. Your task is to cleverly respond.

2. You seem to switch jobs a lot. Why? The wrong answer, of course, is simply to say you're always on the lookout for a better job with better pay. Nobody's going to hire a candidate who so clearly sees every position as a stepping stone to the next. It is reasonable to change employers after three years or so because a new opportunity has arisen that is not possible with your current firm. Anything less than three years requires a convincing explanation. Acceptable reasons for switching employment are downsizing, job situation, career advancement, back to school or a temporary personal situation. These days being a trailing spouse (the spouse who gives up their job to follow their spouse's job change) is acceptable as long as you can convince the HR person you (and your spouse) are here to stay.

3. What would you change about your former job? Never speak negatively about your former position, co-workers or supervisor. If you're asked about a former job, use the opportunity to express how you wished you could have had more responsibilities, or that you wanted to become a more valuable member of the team. Seeking additional opportunities to rise to the occasion on a job demonstrates admirable initiative, something employers like and seek.

4. Where would you like to be in your career five years from now? This is difficult because no one can foretell the future, but if you consider the promotions you might earn if you work hard for the company you're applying to, it's conceivable that you might be able to broadly sketch new duties or status. The important thing here is to emphasize that you plan to be at the company for years to come.

Do not answer with "I want your job." With few exceptions, such as retiring, no one is anxious to hire someone who is gunning to take their position. A better answer might be something like, "I would like to work toward a job similar to yours." It sounds much less threatening, but says the same thing, and sounds respectful to the interviewer.

5. What's an example of a major problem you faced and overcame? Here's a terrific moment for a CAR story, one that relates to an event in your work career, at school or civic activity. Remember to deliver the story in a thorough, compelling manner. Provide important details. Avoid anything that would confuse the central theme of your tale, which is how you conquered a problem. This kind of question is asked by interviewers who want to observe how you define a problem, identify options, decide on a solution, manage obstacles and solve predicaments. It is always nice to end a tale with what you learned from the experience and why you are now a better potential employee for the company.

6. What has been your greatest accomplishment? What did you learn from it? Here is where a personal anecdote might actually serve well. While recounting how you saved your company $1 million in taxes might be quite an achievement, it will ring false in terms of personal accomplishment. It suggests you have no life outside work. Better to mention your marriage, the birth of a child or how you helped someone in need. One anecdote that I encourage college students to emphasize is that you worked full-time to put yourself through college. Talk about an example of hard work and perseverance. The details in your answer can be used to reveal attractive elements of you the person and what traits you will bring to the job.

On the other hand, this is not the time to talk about overcoming drug abuse, alcoholism or failed marriages. Way too personal and alarming. That's a whole different book.

7. What was your greatest failure? What did you learn? Fessing up to failure shows maturity. Everybody fails. It's a law of physics. Of course, don't cite a failure that is so breathtaking that the interviewer forgets everything else about you. Avoid examples that might reflect upon your ability to do the job or could potentially reflect poorly upon your character. A good example might be a fear of speaking in public that prompted you to join Toastmasters. As a result, you're now quite comfortable giving presentations. Such an example illustrates not just that you're human (we all have flaws) but that you've successfully acted to fix a shortcoming. Another example might be how you unsuccessfully attempted to play professional football with disastrous or hilarious consequences, but then turned that experience into a career as a sports attorney.

8. What is your greatest weakness? Again focus on work, not your personal life or character. Turn this question from a negative to a positive by showing how your commitment to work sometimes translates into working long hours, sacrificing free time to get the job done. You might note, for example, that you've become much more organized and now prioritize better so that essential projects are always completed on time.

9. What motivates you to do a good job? Don't say "money." While we all work for a paycheck, no employer wants to hear it—especially from someone who doesn't even have the job yet. A better answer might be that you're motivated to tackle challenges and overcome them, that you draw deep satisfaction from doing every job well. A second reply might be that you like new challenges. The better you do on current projects, the more likely you will be given new opportunities to learn new skills.

10. Have you ever been fired from a job? If so, why? Be honest. It's difficult to hide one's work history for long, and doing so will always come back to bite you. Remember that being laid off doesn't necessarily reflect poorly upon you. Between mergers, outsourcing and new technologies, lots of good people are being allowed the opportunity to find challenges elsewhere.

If you were fired from a job for reasons related to personality differences, it's okay to say so, but be ready to explain why and what you learned from it. Often the personalities and work styles of good supervisors and good employees don't mesh and there may be no way to resolve the conflict in-house. So someone has to go. If it was you, it's only fair that you explain the situation to an inquiring potential employer who would want to make sure such a situation would not be repeated. That's to your benefit as well.

11. Have you ever been convicted of a crime? It's legal to ask this question if it has a bearing on the job you're seeking. A bank, for example, would not want to hire a convicted robber or embezzler to work in the vault. If you have a conviction, it's best to admit it, explain what happened, and any mitigating circumstances. It is essential that you discuss how the experience has made you a better person and what you've done to make amends. For example, if you were convicted of using drugs as a teen, explain

 ## Real (and Really Dumb) Questions

Actually asked during interviews:
- What is it that you people do at this company?
- Why aren't you in a more interesting business?
- What are the zodiac signs of all the board members?
- Why do you want references?
- Do I have to dress for the next interview?
- I know this is off the subject, but will you marry me?
- Will the company move my rock collection from California to Maryland?
- Will the company pay to relocate my horse?
- Does your health insurance cover pets?
- Would it be a problem if I'm angry most of the time?
- Does your company have a policy regarding concealed weapons?
- Do you think the company would be willing to lower my pay?
- Why am I here?

how you went to a rehab facility, got clean and learned how to make better friends and choices. Basically you acknowledged the weakness, conquered it and learned from it.

Checklist

Every job interview is unique. There are basic themes and experiences central to all, of course, but the details vary in every situation. The one thing common to them all is you, though even you are changing and adapting as needed.

No one has yet concocted an absolute, foolproof guide to conducting the perfect job interview. It's just not possible. Still, what follows is my checklist of things to do and think about before, during and after an interview. Follow them. Add to the list. It will serve you well:

- Strive to be the last interview for an open position. This can be tricky. But if you know a company is interviewing several candidates, it's better to be interviewed later than sooner. You will be fresher in mind when the hiring decision is made. How do you do this? If they say they are interviewing Wednesday and Thursday, ask for Thursday afternoon.
- Do your homework before the interview. Know what questions are likely to be asked and what your answers will be. Have questions of your own. Research the company and be able to discuss its product mix and goals.
- Look and behave with respect, seriousness and a positive attitude.
- Listen more than you speak, but stay engaged in the conversation.
- Take notes, if possible. It's a good way to remember names and details for later correspondence and follow-up.
- Use humor smartly. Poke fun only at yourself. Never be sarcastic. Don't force it. If the interviewer is being deadly serious, follow their lead. When in doubt, play it straight.

I Want the Job!

A final bit of advice, which might seem obvious but is often, appallingly, not followed. As your job interview winds down or comes to an end, there will be a moment for you to make a statement.

That statement should say something to this effect: "Thank you for this opportunity. I'm excited about the prospect of working here. I really want this job!"

Telling a would-be employer that you want the job would seem to be a "no-duh!" suggestion, but I can tell you that I've been in hundreds of interviews where that sentiment was never expressed. I've met scores of candidates who have worked hard to get a job interview. They've smartly conducted that interview, impressed HR with their skill set, their work experience and what they could bring to the position and company. But they never say they want the job.

It's not a small point or minor oversight. Employers want to be convinced that the person they're hiring wants the job, that getting it is Job #1 for them. The best, fastest way to persuade a prospective employer is to express that priority in clear, concise, compelling terms.

Of course, you have to mean it. If you don't think a job is right for you, if you're no longer interested, you should say so. Not at the job interview; be gracious. Thank them for their time and consideration, then withdraw your candidacy the next day.

But if you want the job, tell the person!

Sue's personal passion involves working with kids whose lives are a constant struggle due to poverty, abuse, illness or other similar reasons. One day, after years of counseling thousands of clients to find their ideal job, Sue realized she wasn't practicing what she preached.

There is a wonderful children's organization in San Diego that had an opening for a senior development person, someone responsible for finding new ways to support and expand the center's mission and good works.

Normally, Sue would take news of the opening and talk to clients whom she thought might be suitable or interested candidates. Instead, we had a conversation about the job opening and concluded that it was time for her to pursue her own passions—and this job seemed to be ideal.

I knew two of the center's directors and referred Sue for the job. Never underestimate the power of a personal reference. Sue almost immediately got a call from the center's HR manager setting up a telephone interview. Anxious to learn more about the job but thinking it already sounded perfect, Sue quickly agreed to an interview the next afternoon.

Like most of us, Sue is a very busy person. The following day proved to be heavily booked. Sue had inadequate time to prepare and was racing home from a client session that had run long when her cell phone rang.

It was the center's HR manager calling a bit early. He wondered if they could chat. It was hard to say no though there were plenty of reasons to do so. Among them: Sue was driving and all of her notes about the center, its goals, and her thoughts about the job were sitting on her desk at home.

Of course, Sue said she was happy to talk, even with the mobile phone connection dropping three times during the interview.

It was nerve-wracking, but being a consummate professional (she trains people how to do interviews), Sue managed. Indeed, she got a call back for a second interview with senior management and a third with the staff of the development department.

The learning points here are about preparation. Expect the unexpected. Prepare for the worst. Take charge if you can. Schedule your interviews with plenty of time for unforeseen events like a request by an interviewer to stick around to talk with others in the company about the job. Keep relevant materials handy. And if you do get caught in your car or another less-than-conducive place for an interview, say so. Ask the interviewer if you can call them back when you're not driving or when you've found a quieter location. It shows you value the interview and want to ensure it's productive and free of distractions for everyone involved.

 ## Real (and Really Weird) Things Said During Interviews

- I have no difficulty in starting or holding my bowel movement.
- At times, I have the strong urge to do something harmful or shocking.
- I feel uneasy indoors.
- Sometimes I feel like smashing things.
- Women should not be allowed to drink in cocktail bars.
- I think that Lincoln was greater than Washington.
- I get excited very easily.
- Once a week, I usually feel hot all over.
- I am fascinated by fire.
- I like tall women.
- People are always watching me.
- Almost everyone is guilty of bad sexual conduct.
- I must admit that I am a pretty fair talker.
- I never get hungry.
- I know who is responsible for most of my troubles.
- If the pay were right, I'd travel with the carnival.
- I would have been more successful if nobody had snitched on me.
- My legs are really hairy.
- I think I'm going to throw up.

phil•osophy 101 ██7

The other big black hole.

The first black hole is the place your résumé goes after you send it to HR—apparently never to be heard or seen again. Then, miracle of miracles, you're summoned for an interview, the interview you labored so hard and long to get. You meet the hiring manager and have a fantastic session. You hit every talking point and believe you made a great impression. Heck, the manager even said so, promising to get back to you very, very soon. Wink, wink.

Enter the black hole.

A question I hear repeatedly from job candidates is how long should they wait after an interview before pressing the hiring manager for a decision. Or just an update. If you haven't heard back from a company within two weeks of a final interview, there's a good chance one or more of the following is happening:

- *You're not the only candidate being considered. The company is talking to others, and it may be taking a while for all of these interviews to be scheduled and conducted.*

- *The decision-makers at the company are having difficulty coming to an actual decision. It might be as simple as the fact that it's a committee choice and the committee is having trouble getting everybody together. It may also be that the decision-makers are traveling and can't get together to make the decision.*

- *Maybe it's just a tough choice. Maybe you're not the company's first choice, but your application is strong enough that HR doesn't want to cut you loose just yet. If choice #1 doesn't work out, HR wants to keep you close by and available.*

- *Or perhaps the job situation has changed. After conducting several interviews, it's possible the hiring manager's view of the open position has changed. He or she thinks the job specifications need to be altered, upgraded or shifted. While that's going on, everything's been put on hold. Now, with all of the interviews done, the decision-makers are reconsidering the job description, the compensation package (up or down) or the experience/education requirements. You and your peers gave them feedback that made them wonder about their current criteria for the job.*

These are all viable reasons for a company to step back and not rush a hiring decision, which isn't much consolation to you, left hanging there. In this chapter, we'll talk about what you can do during this excruciating period in the hiring process. This is the time to show your professional patience, rather than reveal any frustrations or, heaven forbid, lose your temper. Display your understanding of this wrinkle in the HR process and you may further impress those HR folks and the people you hope to work with. Let other candidates flail and fume; your job is to remain focused on getting the job.

Congratulations, you've got the job

7

"Every day I get up and look through the *Forbes* list of the richest people in America. If I'm not there, I go to work."
—ROBERT ORBEN

"In business, you don't get what you deserve, you get what you negotiate."
—CHESTER L. KARRASS

"Many people quit looking for work when they find a job."
—AUTHOR UNKNOWN

The big job interview is over; your job is not.

Take a deep breath. This is not a sigh of relief. It's in preparation for the next step.

Oh sure, you've come a long way, working hard to do those early self-assessments, establish networks, write résumés, make phone calls, pound the pavement. It has been a labor that would exhaust Hercules. Your reward was the job interview you wanted and needed.

Now it's time to seal the deal.

The period after a job interview can be maddening. Job candidates often feel ignored, abandoned, left to wander in a desert of doubt and disquiet. (Is that piece of paper that's drifting in the wind your application?)

Unless HR or the person doing the hiring has clearly and explicitly laid out a timetable for the decision-making process (something that's rarely done, and even less often accurate), it's likely you'll be left to wonder what's happening until something actually happens.

This might seem like a time of relative powerlessness. The decision to hire you or not is now in the hands of others. While that's indisputably true, you can still do a lot to influence the final result. Until you receive word that a final choice has been made, you must continue to campaign for the job. Your goal is to make a connection with your target person or audience every ten working days until resolution, to remind them of your interest and re-emphasize just how perfectly suited you are to the open position.

The first step should be obvious: the post-interview thank you note. We covered thank you notes in Chapter 5.

Once your thank you is signed, sealed and delivered, you begin the art and practice of polite persistence. You want to stay in contact with HR and on their collective minds. This can be achieved in many ways.

One of the best is to keep sending notes on a regular basis. These shouldn't be empty gestures that merely show you're still alive and available. They should be indications that you are already, in a sense, working for the company. For example, find an article that you think the hiring manager would find interesting or relevant. Send a note or email with the material attached.

Most often, it will be work-related, but you can also send items that simply reflect something you think the recipient will appreciate. Perhaps during the job interview, the hiring manager mentioned that she enjoys reading histories of medieval England and you notice that such a book has hit the bestseller lists with fine reviews. Send along a note with a review attached. It's a nice gesture that can only elevate your status in the hiring manager's eyes—even if she knows why you're doing it (and she probably does).

Notice here I did not say buy a copy of the book and deliver it. HR folks are very sensitive about what might be considered an unseemly gift, or even a bribe. The offering of a book might be intended merely as an act of thoughtfulness, but it can be construed as a gift intended to purchase beneficial consideration. It could put the recipient in an uncomfortable position. More than likely, the HR recipient would have to send the book back and that would be awkward for everyone.

In talking about sending notes, it might sound like I'm suggesting you do this only when you stumble across something relevant to your interview. Quite the opposite. Don't let happenstance dictate your career. If you've just interviewed with the HR person who loves histories of medieval England, go looking for interesting items you can use to re-connect. Visit a bookstore to see what sorts of similar novels are on the market. Surf the web. Find out what's out there and what people are saying or writing about the subject, then use the fruits of your labor to further your cause.

Written notes are one way to maintain contact, but not the only way. You can call or even drop by, but do so only if you have a good, solid, plausible reason. Dropping by to just say "hi" is not sufficient. It's just wasting time—yours and theirs—and it might be perceived as a little weird and off-putting.

Similarly, keep your contacts professional. Sending work-relevant articles or observations is a good thing; sending cookies is not. Remember you are not their personal friend—yet. Keep all of your contacts businesslike and above-board. Never mention families or personal life. Don't come across as a stalker. You never want to risk making them feel uncomfortable with you.

Doing all of the above doesn't necessarily eliminate the stress and angst of waiting to find out whether you got a job or not, but it just helps. At least you feel like you are engaged and working to make something happen. If you were the decision-maker, wouldn't you be impressed with the candidate that enthusiastically told you that he or she wanted the job and, very professionally, stayed in touch with you? Especially if all the other candidates left the interview never to be heard from again.

And you should always keep in mind the old adage about not putting all of your eggs (and effort) in one basket. If you've interviewed for your "dream job," fantastic! Work the angles. Do everything you can to achieve success. But don't stop looking elsewhere. Maintain your networks, line up other interviews, press forward on multiple fronts.

I've seen too many candidates do the job interview, then sit back to await word. Weeks pass. Then they come to me and say, "It's been two months and the company hasn't made a decision."

Yes it has. It just didn't tell you.

So when you think your candidacy is not getting the attention you think it deserves, what do you do? Last ditch is to contact the hiring manager and tell them you have another job offer followed quickly by "but your position at Company A really interests me. When do you think you will be making a decision?" This approach does one of two things: It kicks companies into fear (for fear of losing you) or gives them an easy out to say "take the other job."

If Company A was just putting off telling you that you are not getting the job offer then the technique worked to finally get closure. If they really want you, then it got them into gear. Either action works for you. The difficult situation is if they say, "Thank you for telling us. You are still a viable candidate for the position but we are not ready to make a decision yet." Tell them that you can hold off for two more weeks; the game continues. They know there is a clock ticking. Offer to get back with them in a week for an update if you have not heard anything.

The Other Perspective

One theme I've tried to hit again and again is that there's more than one perspective to any job-seeking enterprise. There's the viewpoint of the applicant, of course, which is critical. But even more critical is the perspective of the employer who, after all, is the one with the job opening.

Let's talk a bit about how employers view the job offer that they just gave you, which for them is almost as big a moment as it is for the applicant. Maybe more so since they will be investing measurable resources in this person.

Odds are the employer has gone through a fairly extensive, rigorous process to find the person they think is right for the job. Someone in HR (maybe many people) has combed through résumés, conducted interviews and research and done much, much more to get to find...you.

Now they want to make the job offer and close the deal. A few things may be guiding their thought process at this point: 1) Difficulty in filling the position and other candidates. 2) Speed of closure. 3) Standard contract. 4) No outliers. 5) Long-term potential.

What do these things mean to you?

1. If finding the right person for the job—you—was the result of a long, hard process, that bodes well for you in negotiating the terms of your employment. On the other hand, if there are a lot of other suitable candidates in the wings, you shouldn't play hard-to-get.
2. Once a job offer is made, most employers want to wrap things up quickly. There are other things to do, other open jobs to fill.
3. Most companies have a standard employment contract (assuming they have a written contract) and prefer to stick as closely as possible to it. It's simpler. It's what they know and understand best. However, most companies also realize that a standard contract is not etched in stone. It's the basis for negotiation and can be changed. They're just likely to want to change it as little as possible.
4. No outliers means they don't want to negotiate and approve an employment agreement with you that is dramatically or radically different from agreements with other employees. Don't ask for a salary double what your peers make. The company wants a level playing field, with equitable benefits so that everybody's equally happy—or unhappy.
5. How long will you be with the company? Every HR manager will ask that question, both internally and to you. Your answer, naturally, is just short of forever. You are a long-term solution. HR wants to believe that too, so they don't have to find your replacement in six months.

Hold Your Horses

The moment arrives.

You get the call.

You're offered the job.

You want the job.

You want to say yes.

Hold your horses.

Never accept a proffered position until you've had time to consider a few things. These include, naturally, issues like salary and benefits, but also might include things like commute time, office space, childcare, weekend work and how much time you'll be away from home or family.

Most job offers don't come out of the blue. By the time you've finished a job interview, you should have a pretty good notion of what the job entails, what it pays and how it's likely to impact your career and life. Nonetheless, these issues cannot be fully evaluated until you have a legitimate job offer or employment agreement in hand.

And to do that, you need time—at the very least a few days, quite often more.

Asking for time to consider a job offer is fair and reasonable. You can do so by simply saying you need to discuss the offer's details with your spouse or family. No employer should deny you this opportunity, and few would. If a would-be employer does, it's a red flag and you should immediately ask why an immediate decision is required. You might want to seriously reconsider whether you want to work there. A demand that you decide here and now suggests the company places its interests first and foremost, without real regard to employee rights or considerations.

No matter what the work, a job offer is a thing of many parts. It may be fairly simple or extremely complex. It may consist of only a few pages of paperwork that you can work through by yourself or require multiple binders and the assistance of a lawyer or employment professional.

I'll get into some specifics in a moment, but here are some quick rules of thumb for working out an employment agreement:

1. The job offer or employment agreement must be in writing.
2. Negotiate at the time of the job offer, not before.
3. Read and understand all of the documents involved. Take your time.
4. Review documents or agreements with a lawyer, mentor or someone whose judgment you value and trust.
5. At the very least, review and discuss the agreement with HR.
6. Request a reasonable amount of time to review any documents.

7. Everything can be discussed, everything may be negotiable.
8. Strive for an agreement that is reasonable, clear, brief and complete.
9. Focus on the items most important to you. Negotiate hard for these items. Concede items that aren't important.
10. Don't end your job search or eliminate other opportunities until you've actually started your new job.

When you get a job offer, take it home and analyze it. You want to see if it really meets all of your needs. You want to see if it contains elements that cause pause or which you might later regret. You want to balance the positives (big salary, company car) against the negatives (limited medical benefits, working weekends).

You want to understand every aspect of a job offer. Nothing should come as a surprise later on. ("What does 'indentured servant' mean?") If you're confused about some part of the offer, ask for clarification from HR or, if appropriate, an outside entity like a lawyer.

The first thing almost everybody thinks about when considering a job is salary. How much does the job pay? That's understandable. It's why we work. Everybody needs money. As Woody Allen once observed, "Money is better than poverty, if only for financial reasons."

Salary tends to be the Number One issue for most job applicants. In some cases, that's known going in and may be non-negotiable, though you can inquire if you think there's reasonable room and cause for discussion.

The offer you get will likely depend upon a number of factors, some based on you and your qualifications, others on the nature of the company and industry. These include:

- Your work experience. More experience, more money.
- The market rate for your position. Companies keep a close eye on what competitors are paying employees. They want to offer attractive salaries, not excessive ones.
- The nature of the work. Is this job one of a hundred just like it or singular? How many people can do the work? How many have applied for the position?
- The nature of the company. Some businesses and industries have fairly rigid salary schedules. They're locked in by union contracts, business customs or plain old inertia. Young firms may be more flexible and open-minded than older companies that have been doing things a certain way for a long time.

When a company finally makes a salary offer, always consider making a counteroffer, particularly if you think it's reasonable and you have compelling, persuasive arguments to back it up.

It's hard to know how much a company is willing to pay, but almost invariably a first offer is at least slightly less than the maximum. (By the way, if any CEO or HR Manager asks me about this I will deny that I ever said it!)

If you think you're worth more than the first offer and want to counter, do your homework first. Find out what your value is in the job market. You might already have a good idea if you've been doing a certain kind of work for a while, but don't hesitate to go beyond that for new information, advice and tips. Look at job board listings describing similar positions. Use salary calculators at various job-related websites, such as CareerBuilding.com or Monster.com. Payscale.com, for example, offers pay analysis comparing your job profile to the salary and compensation packages of people whose skills and experience match with yours. And Salary.com provides on-demand compensation management, information on pay and benefits, as well as performance and salary data. Users can research the assessed worth of their position based on job title and ZIP code searches. Cost-of-living calculators and salary differentials are also offered.

If you're inexperienced or fretful about compensation negotiations, don't be reluctant to seek guidance and help. If you have a trusted mentor, ask for advice. Be wary of family or friends, however, who may have your best interests at heart, but no real insight or knowledge about negotiating salary and benefits.

Most of all, think long and hard about how you make a counteroffer. The last thing you want a new employer to think is that it's just about money—and that you view the offered salary to be inadequate. You worked hard and successfully to get this job, to convince your new boss that you will be an exemplary employee driven by real interest in the work and upstanding values. Don't undermine that perception by immediately asking for more money unless you know for a fact that you can make a solid, persuasive, fact-based case for bumping it up.

Far better to take the job, work hard and earn a pay raise later. Speaking of negotiating skills:

I once had a manager for another Manpower franchise contact me about job opportunities at our operation in San Diego. At the time, she worked at the largest and most respected Manpower franchise so I was really interested in the possibility of her joining our team. I thought we could learn a lot from her about how to grow our business and become even more successful.

After various discussions and interviews, I thought she seemed like the ideal person to head a new "permanent placement division" and I offered her our normal starting package. She paused, pointed out that her years of experience merited a much higher salary and that the new job she was being asked to do warranted additional compensation. I told her that my offer was our normal package and I wasn't accustomed to negotiating.

Her reply: "Don't you want me to negotiate as hard on your behalf when you hire me as I am now on my behalf?" Wow! She was absolutely right. I suddenly realized that her years of experience were probably worth what she was asking for and that the unprecedented duties deserved unprecedented compensation. The epiphany for me was not to simply rule out counteroffers. Period, no discussion. It's up to job candidates to put forth serious, reasonable, valid reasons for increased compensation packages. It's up to people like me to give them serious consideration. I agreed with her arguments and wound up hiring her because of her negotiating skills. We're both happy.

To be sure, salary is almost always just part of the total "compensation package." There are many other elements to consider, including healthcare, education, vacation, retirement and perks like a company car or car allowance. More possibilities are stock options, bonuses, office location options, on-site childcare, in-house exercise facilities, working from home and more.

Not surprisingly, the relative importance of these elements differs among people. Salary may be priority number one for a young, single guy just starting out in business; but healthcare benefits may be more important to a family man or retirement plans to somebody looking at just another few years of work.

Before you sit down with an employer to discuss compensation, sit down with your family and make a list of the benefits that matter most to you. Be fair and reasonable in your assessments. Be prepared to be flexible in discussions.

When you do negotiate, strive to maximize your compensation package without appearing unreasonable or inflexible. This can be a tricky process, demanding equal amounts of smarts, finesse, dexterity, creativity and good faith.

When we poll employees about why they choose to stay with a certain job or decide to leave a company, salary is not their first response. In fact, it is fifth, as you see below. So when you are considering accepting a job offer, use these filters as a way to make sure that this is the right job for you:

- Am I challenged?
- Am I learning new things?
- Am I surrounded by motivating co-workers?
- Am I having fun?
- Am I fairly compensated?

The Complete Package

While every compensation package is different, here are some of the likely elements you might find and need to consider:

- **Health Insurance.** After salary, this is the biggest and most variable part of any compensation package. Unless you privately insure yourself, your employment agreement should include some type of medical and long-term disability insurance. Ideally, it should also offer dental, vision, life and short-term disability (or at least provide the option of buying into these programs through a group rate plan). The harsh reality, alas, is that many companies only offer medical insurance to full-time employees. (Part-timers and contract employees are often left to their own devices.)
- **Whatever your proffered options, pay close attention to them.** If you're confused, ask questions. Learn the differences between preferred providers and HMOs, and which is best for you and your family. Is there a pension plan? A 401K? Does your employer provide any kind of matching money? Your hard work now will pay off later.
- **Bonus or incentive pay.** Is this pay in addition to an acceptable base salary or offered as a way to bulk up a substandard paycheck? If it's the latter, what are the benchmarks for achieving the extra income? Are they reasonable? Are they achievable?
- **Signing bonus.** Unless you're a southpaw with a 100-mile-per-hour fastball, don't expect a signing bonus. They're increasingly rare in the ordinary business world, though you might be able to negotiate

something like a bonus if you're being asked to uproot and move your family across country. Call it a relocation fee.

■ **Previously scheduled time-off.** Let's say you had a long-planned trip with the family to the ancestral homelands. A new job opportunity arises. You go for it. You get it. The new employer is eager for you to start as soon as possible. It's often quite possible to negotiate that time off before you begin the new job—and make sure it isn't deducted from your vacation time with the new company. The request is more common than you think, and most companies will work with new employees if they can. The key is to be upfront and proactive.

■ **Working at home.** Many employees relish the idea. Many companies do too, especially if it helps the bottom line. (A company saves money if it doesn't have to find office space for everybody, every day.) If you want to work at home and it's feasible in your new position, discuss the option. Be clear and specific about why this is a good idea and how it will help the company. Don't forget to ask about reimbursements for costs like your Internet connection, long-distance phone calls, office supplies and postage.

■ **Stock options.** If a company offers these, investigate them in detail. Are they based on performance or paygrade level? Look at their historical market value? Beware of companies that offer you stock options in lieu of salary or benefits. A stock option is only as good as the company offering it. A company that pays with stock options may be giving you worthless paper.

■ **Severance pay.** It seems a little odd to ask about compensation if things go sour, kind of like insisting on a prenuptial agreement with your future spouse. But, hey, this is business. It's not personal. The work world is a tough, volatile place. Things don't always go as you hope and plan. A dream job can become a nightmare. You might find yourself in a depressingly familiar position again—unemployed.

If that happens, you'll be grateful that you discussed severance pay when times were young, beautiful and everybody smiled. Many companies have standard severance packages, which range from a guarantee of at least two weeks' pay to several months. The longer you're with a company, the bigger the severance package should be.

Asking about severance pay might sound unseemly, but it's really not and you should know what might happen if the worst happens.

■ **Non-compete agreements.** Some industries and companies ask new employees to sign an agreement promising that they will not work for a direct competitor for a specific period of time after leaving a job. Usually it's one or two years.They do it to protect themselves. They don't want ex-employees spilling company secrets.

If you're asked to sign a non-compete agreement, think first before you sign. It might be a no-brainer if you figure you'll spend the next 10-15 years at the same company, but if you imagine yourself leaving much sooner, perhaps working for similar companies, it behooves you to go slow. Read the agreement carefully. Make sure it's reasonable and not overly restrictive. If it's the latter, ask for changes—but only if you can reasonably defend them.

■ **Other perks.** Company cars or car allowances, special loans, paid memberships to clubs, enhanced insurance benefits, discounts to local businesses or attractions.

Always keep in mind when the first comp package is offered, there are features that may be of real value to you, but don't cost the employer any more money. These might even be features the employer has never offered before. Some examples are flex time—either hours or days. A 9-to-5 shift may be traditional, but it's hardly written in stone. There are all kinds of work week formulations that might do the job and save you time, money and hassle (like getting to daycare). If you and your employer can work out an arrangement that's mutually beneficial and agreeable, go for it.

Similarly, telecommuting is a growing option for many employers. They save the overhead costs of housing employees; you save the cost of commute time and expense. With gas regularly surging past $4 a gallon, it's a measurable benefit not to have to drive to work every day.

Making the Hard Decision

Getting a job offer might seem like a slam-dunk decision, but sometimes it is not. It can be a moment of great importance. I've known countless job applicants who worked assiduously to line up a job, only to balk at the moment it was offered.

A little balkiness is natural. A new job means venturing into the unknown, and that gives most people at least some pause. But what about applicants who seem to do and say all the right things to get a job, then suddenly don't seem all that interested when it's offered to them?

Usually the reason is not a surprise: The job was never right for them—and they were never right for the job. Confronted with the opportunity, they suddenly see reasons why they shouldn't seize it. Those reasons were always there. They just didn't recognize them.

Before you take a job, weigh the intangibles. Some of them you should already have pondered earlier in the job-hunting process when you were plotting what kind of work you wanted to do. Earlier in this chapter I talked about what employees said made for a fulfilling job situation. Now, its crunch time for the job offer. Opportunity has knocked. Are you going to answer?

Ask yourself these questions (again):

- Do you want to learn new skills? Does this job teach them?
- Is this job a stepping stone on a longer career path?
- Does this job give you more authority and/or responsibility? Do you want them?
- Will you be challenged? Do you want to be challenged?
- Do you want to work alone or as part of a team?
- Are you looking for a position with less stress?
- Do you want to work in a fast-moving, high-growth industry?
- What kind of job security do you need?
- How important is pay, title or perks?
- What about overtime, travel, working weekends?
- How will the new job affect life at home? How does your family view it?

These, of course, are only a few questions you might reasonably ask yourself. Depending upon the particulars of the job and your circumstances, there are many, many others. The point is to have a serious discussion with yourself (and others) so that when you make your decision, you know exactly why and can live with it.

Your First Day

When you get to this point, you've almost arrived. There is always more work to do, which is why there are two more chapters after this one. Your first day of work marks the end of one process and the beginning of a new one.

We'll go into greater detail about what happens after Day One at the new job, but first let's discuss how to tie up a few loose ends and get things off to a fabulous start. The basics are really pretty easy, and mirror some of the things you've learned and done to get this far.

A first day at work is a lot like going to a job interview. You want to adequately prepare. If possible, know what will be expected of you when you walk in the door that first time. Be on time. Look good. Dress appropriately. Smile and greet others warmly. These are your co-workers. First impressions count, and relationships often bloom or die based on first impressions.

First days are often a whir of new names and faces, most of which you fear you'll never remember. You will, but more importantly, remember this: Everybody you meet may play a big part in your unfolding career. A co-worker today could be your boss tomorrow. Or vice versa. Treat them all with dignity and respect.

As you begin to put faces with names, learn as much as you can. Who are the movers and shakers in your department or company? Who are the best and brightest? Who can help you become a better employee and person? Use them as models and mentors.

Finally, go for it. You may be the new guy or gal, but now is not the time to be shy. Ask questions. Seek responsibility. If your new boss is looking for volunteers, step up. The learning curve might be steeper and harder, but you'll get to the top of the hill faster.

phil•osophy 101

8

This chapter really brings together two overarching thoughts.

The first is a variation on the line from Walt Kelly's celebrated cartoon character Pogo, who wryly opined, "We have met the enemy and he is us."

As I mentioned before, we all have a Career Manager and he is us. Our Career Manager exists not just to help find us a job. He (or she) is also there to guide us when we have a job. My point: Your work doesn't end when you find work. Never stop thinking about your career, both what's happening in the moment and what will happen next. All of the work you did to get your current, fabulous position now transitions into labors to keep and excel at this job. We often forget that as an employee our relationship with our employer is only as secure as how essential we are perceived to that employer's success. If management thinks you're not critical to the equation, then you're vulnerable to being tagged as excess, an overhead cost that can be cut. We are all temps! Never forget it.

Similarly, you're likely to remain with a company or employer only as long as you find the position rewarding, both financially and intellectually. Your personal Career Manager should always have his radar out, looking for new challenges for you. The challenge can be within the company you work or outside.

Always keep this radar turned on, not only in terms of detecting new opportunities over the horizon, but in staying on top of changing conditions at work. That's not to say every job is an immediate stepping stone to the next, but you should start actively searching for your next opportunity when either you or your employer begin to feel a lack of value in your working partnership. You want to always be in the posi-tion of quitting, not being fired.

Watch the caliber of new hires coming into your department. If their skill levels are way above yours, then you may be getting stale. You risk being perceived at the "old way of doing things." This is your red flag to upgrade your skills as fast as you can, to do whatever it takes.

If your company is hiring lower-skilled workers, then be aware that you may be overqualified for the job, probably more expensive, and the work you have been doing is ready to outsourced or automated. None of this is good for your long-term future in that position in that firm.

With your career management radar working 24/7, there should never be any surprises in your career, except maybe the pleasant kind.

"The harder I work, the luckier I get." We've all heard stories about people who seemed to be the recipients (deserving or not) of incredible luck. They were at a party and heard cocktail chatter about a fantastic job opportunity. They fortuitously knew a guy who knew a guy, etc.

The first century Roman philosopher Seneca said, "Luck is what happens when preparation meets opportunity." A lot of folks have echoed that sentiment over the millennia. Luck favors those who don't depend upon it. Sure, some things are mostly about luck. Las Vegas comes to mind. But mostly, we must make our own luck by taking advantage of every opportunity we recognize or create.

If you think you're lucky, you'll be lucky. The lucky guy who heard about the dream job at the party may have been lucky because he knew that party was a good place to pick up tips for new opportunities. He was in the right place at the right time because he put himself there. Be that guy. Reach out to people. Attend events. Be seen as personable, interactive and maybe even a little aggressive (but in a good, non-threatening way).

Odds are, you won't get lucky finding a job sitting at a computer all day scrolling employment listings. Computers don't hire people. So put yourself out there. It may be uncomfortable or awkward, but truth be told, it is for almost everyone. Not every outing will pay off immediately or at all. Some ventures will feel like a waste of time. Some might be. But work every opportunity as best you can. It will eventually pay off.

The harder you work, the luckier you will get. If you don't know that by now, ask your Career Manager.

Phil

8   Keeping a job

"Hard work never killed anyone, but why take a chance."
— EDGAR BERGEN

"I always arrive late to the office, but make up for it by always leaving early."
— CHARLES LAMB

"Nobody notices what I do. Until I don't do it."
— A COFFEE MUG

Work is more than just work. It defines who we are.

For one thing, like it or not, it fundamentally determines how we live. I want to be Matt Lauer, hobnobbing daily with the world's most powerful and interesting people, but that's not my job. Likewise, the fellow who sits behind a desk 9-to-5, Monday through Friday, can believe with all of his heart he has the soul of an explorer, but in fact, he's an accountant and will remain so unless he changes jobs and realities.

A major theme of this book has been about defining what kind of job you desire and how to get it recognizing, of course, that in these tough times, just getting a job may be the number one goal, and that's okay in the short term.

What happens, though, once you've landed the job? Your first day at a new job is bound to be exciting, fraught with expectation, high hopes and maybe a little uncertainty. It's the days that follow, however, that will determine whether your job—and career—are successful.

What does that mean—career success? The answer is completely subjective. For all people some of the time and some people all of the time, it is measured in terms of salary, perks and acquisitions. A big paycheck, car and house are obvious benchmarks. Have those, and most folks will think you're doing just fine.

But career success—that is, how you measure the value of your work—is also determined by more personal standards and criteria. It is defined by ideals absorbed and developed from family, friends, education, society and life experience.

Part of what makes a dream job dreamy is knowing how to recognize, pursue and achieve the elements of a job that provide rewards not measurable by a paycheck or a purchase. These rewards can change with time, experience and outlook. One of your greatest career challenges is determining your definition of success, what it means to you and how to achieve it. Here are some tips and tools to help.

First off, success takes hard work. Henry David Thoreau once said it comes most often to people too busy to look for it. There's really no secret to it. (Honestly, have you ever met somebody successful who wasn't eager to tell you how they became that way?) Success means always pressing ahead or, to quote the late, great American businesswoman Mary Kay Ash, falling forward.

Woody Allen said 80% of success was just showing up. There's truth in that joke, but success also means knowing why you've showed up, why you're there. To define job and career success, you've got to know why you work. How many of these commonly cited reasons apply to you:

- To earn a living
- To become rich
- To help others
- To leave a mark in history
- To travel
- To become famous
- To develop skills
- To learn new things
- To become an expert
- To pursue personal interests
- To make the world a better place

If you haven't already done so, now is the time to make a career plan. I'm not talking about fuzzy notions in your head. I'm talking about a living document that you can use as a guide, reminder and source of inspiration. It should be in writing. It should be accessible, something you look at from time to time, amending as needed.

It doesn't have to be elaborate or fancy. It doesn't have to have all of the answers. In fact, it never will. It is just a start, a map to a finish line that you will likely move again and again.

■　■　■

Ed Vargo once joked about his chosen profession: "We're supposed to be perfect our first day on the job, and then show constant improvement." That's remarkably insightful for a major league umpire.

So what exactly constitutes the perfect employee?

Really, it's anybody's guess. Maybe there's no such thing, but it's very clear from numerous surveys of employers, job advisors and college counselors what the top qualities are:

1. Communication skills
2. Strong work ethic
3. Ability to work in a team
4. Initiative
5. Interpersonal skills

You'll notice this list doesn't say intelligence. That's too common. There are lots of smart people out there. You're one of them. You got the job. Now, you need to stay smart, get smarter. That means keeping up-to-date on what's happening in your world of work, and using that knowledge to make yourself a better employee.

Employers look for people who can listen as well as talk, who have the ability to communicate with others both orally and in writing, who know how to manage themselves, make decisions, solve problems, learn new skills, lead and more.

These are not just desired attributes, they are essential to continued success and reaching your goals. If the work world was ever easy (and I'm not sure it was), it is not now. The labor force is shrinking and aging, but also hanging onto jobs longer because people can't afford to retire. Some industries are experiencing radical restructuring. Jobs are disappearing or changing. Old skill sets are becoming obsolete. New skill sets demand abilities unimagined just a few years ago. Job security and employee longevity are virtually gone. Most Americans today figure to have five or six steady, full-time jobs in their lifetimes, maybe two or three different careers. Getting a job is hard work. Keeping a job may be even harder.

Job Won, Day One and Beyond

You've got the job. It's time to go to work. First days and weeks on a new job are usually at least a little bit nerve-wracking. Everything's new and mostly unknown, from colleagues to specific duties to where the restrooms are. Feeling a bit overwhelmed and scared is natural and probably good. Don't worry about it too much. You got the job. You beat out everybody else. They wanted you!

The trick is to make sure your bosses don't think they've made a mistake. The first few weeks and months of a new job are critical to success. First impressions count, so do second and third ones. All of it combines to build your reputation at work, how people see and think about you.

There are basic elements to making a strong, positive impression on people, first or otherwise. They include appearance, attitude, work habits, attendance, personality, ability to fit in and an evident interest in others.

More specifically:

Good attendance. Maybe if you're a hugely successful, iconic comedian-author-moviemaker, just showing up works. If you're new to a job, shoot for 100%. No, make that 110%.

It's critical to show your dedication early in a new job. To establish a good reputation, you must put in the time. Arrive early, stay late. Your hours may ease as you begin to understand your responsibilities and find ways to do them better in less time, but in the beginning, it's all about not just showing up, but being there.

Learn names and roles quickly. Everybody likes having his or her name remembered. It indicates they've made an impression on you, that they were worth your devoting a few neural circuits to remembering them. You may meet a lot of people. It may be hard to remember all of their names, but try.

■　■　■

If you ask people what their favorite word in the English language is, they will always hesitate and become introspective. Research has shown that our favorite word is our own name. When you meet people, use their name repeatedly as a way to help remember it. When you say good morning to someone, add their name at the beginning or end. You will see them visibly perk up. People appreciate the recognition and familiarity of other people using their names. You will see lots of long-term dividends.

There are lots of ways and resources to improve your memory for names. A quick surf of the Internet reveals scores of websites with advice. Here are a few quick tips:

1. Be interested. Pay conscious attention when first introduced. Don't let the name just wash away.

2. Verify it. Casually repeat the name back. Ask how it's spelled if the name is unusual. If you're at a conference or place where people wear name tags, check the tag. Don't be shy to admit you're just trying to fix that person's name in your head. They'll appreciate the effort.

3. Imagine their name written on their forehead. That was Franklin Roosevelt's favorite mnemonic device. Use different colors of imaginary ink.

4. Write their names in your head. Watch your hand forming the letters.

5. Use word associations. If someone's name is Hattie, imagine them wearing a stack of hats on their head. If their name is Jack, imagine them hammering away outside with a big, noisy pneumatic jack. If their name is Arnold, imagine them saying, "Hasta la vista, baby." Whatever works.

6. As I said, use names frequently. Once you know somebody's name, use it soon and often. Don't be too obvious or obnoxious about it (you don't want to sound like a salesman), but a few uses should get the name into a groove you'll easily recall.

7. Record names in a file you can easily call up, such as a contacts list on your cell phone. Review the file regularly, maybe every time you update it with a new name. Peruse it whenever you anticipate being in a place or situation where you're likely to meet people whose names you should know or remember.

Know your goals. Know what's expected of you. If you don't get one, ask your boss for a job description and where you are expected to be in 30, 60 and 90 days. Are there specific benchmarks, such as skills you must learn or goals you must reach?

Ask questions. Don't assume anything, which as the old saw goes, can make an idiot out of you and me, but also get you fired. It's much easier to ask for instructions now than to explain a mistake later. Listen carefully to answers. Write them down, if necessary. You aren't expected to know everything immediately. People expect you to ask for help. If you don't, they may think you're just not paying attention or worse, you don't really care.

Ask for feedback. Don't be afraid to ask, "How am I doing?" Seek input and guidance from others to ensure you're heading in the right direction, that you're doing things correctly. Fix a mistake before it's a fatal one.

Gather information around you. Be inquisitive and observant. Talk to your colleagues about work, about any "unwritten rules." Learn the inside scoop, but avoid gossip. This is not about being nosy or meddlesome. This is about better understanding your workplace so that you can be as productive as possible.

Stay organized. This means having a system for retaining and using what you know and learn. Create a filing system that works for you. Be realistic about what you can and will do. Don't go out and buy a bank of filing cabinets that will end up ignored, empty and gathering dust somewhere. Start modestly and build up as work demands. Keep a calendar—on your computer, cell phone or in your briefcase. Consult and update it regularly. Write down meetings. Make project plans. Do everything you can to stay on top of what's happening. You'll feel better, more in control and fewer things will fall through the cracks.

Be and stay positive. Leave your personal life at home (and conversely, leave your work life at work). Be enthusiastic at work. It makes everything easier, for you and your co-workers.

Fit in. Don't do or say anything that will make you stand out in a negative way. That includes what you wear, when you come or leave work, when you take lunch, how you behave in meetings and among co-workers. There will be time and opportunity to express your individuality.

Be a team player. Make the effort (extra or not) to help whenever you can. People want to see if you can fit into and work in a group. The best way to prove you can is to reach out to others. Be flexible. Follow the lead of others. You must become part of the pack before you can become the leader of it.

Avoid or minimize personal business. Your job is where you do your job, not where you buy stuff online, call family and friends or make party plans for the weekend. Do these things on your own time after work, during lunch or scheduled breaks.

Practice the 80/20 rule. Listen 80% of the time, talk 20%. If you talk too much, you're likely to find others tuning you out, especially if you're too free with irrelevant opinions. In fact, avoid opining if at all possible. Stick to research and facts versus feelings and unsubstantiated observations and hearsay.

Don't act like you know it all. You may have been hired because you possess a rare and impressive set of skills, but don't put it all out there immediately for everybody to appreciate. They won't. A few days or months aren't nearly enough to establish you as the consummate expert, unless of course you were hired precisely to fill that position. But even then, be modest. Offer your knowledge and expertise confidently, but with some humility. We can all learn from others.

Read company literature and rules. It may be boring. There may be a lot of it. But it's important for you to be a student of your company. You should understand what your company does and how it seeks to position itself among competitors and in the world. Annual reports and sales brochures are good sources of information and insight.

Surviving (and Thriving) in the Workplace

No two places of employment are alike. That's obviously true when comparing an auto body shop to a hair salon, but it also applies to companies and businesses in the same line of work. A bank is not a bank is not a bank. Bank of America is not the same working environment as Credit Swiss. Every workplace has its own rules, types of people and challenges. The quicker you figure out how your new workplace works, the better you will do. Be a good observer and a better participant. The first few months are all about blending in. You can spread your feathers when you feel comfortable that you are on firm ground.

Let's start with a consideration of "corporate culture." What precisely does that mean? Per Wikipedia, it "describes the psychology, attitudes, experiences, beliefs and values (personal and cultural) of an organization." It has been defined as "the specific collection of values and norms that are shared by people and groups in an organization and that control the way they interact with each other and with stakeholders outside the organization."

In other words, corporate culture is "how things get done around here."

And that clearly affects you. A company's culture/system/routine will dictate or influence:

- The number of hours you work per day or per week, and whether you're required to put in traditional eight-hour days or can choose options like flextime or telecommuting.
- The environment in which you work, whether it's competitive or collegial, formal or relaxed, nose-to-the-grindstone or fun.
- The dress code, what's acceptable, whether there are casual days. What exactly defines "casual?"

■ The way you communicate with colleagues. Are there lots of regularly sched- uled meetings or are decisions made ad hoc in hallways. We all know companies whose style is to email the person in the next cubicle. How do you interact with management? Is there an open door policy? Is there a hierarchy, with lots of gatekeepers between you and the top managers?

■ Your office space. Will you have an office, a cubicle or just a desk in a sea of desks? Are there doors on the offices? Do people get win- dows? Can you display personal items?

■ Your development opportunities. Does the company run training programs for advancement? Can you attend professional confer- ences? Are there ways to improve yourself to make you a better employee and more marketable for future jobs and employers?

■ The perks available. Some companies are rich with them: onsite gyms, daycare facilities and such. Often the abundance and variety of perks is a reflection of how well an industry and companies are doing, or how competitive and creative it must be to attract and keep high-quality employees.

Think about corporate culture like you think about buying a car. You want a car that's comfortable, matches your personal style and lasts long enough to get you where you want to go. A car that doesn't meet these requirements isn't a good fit. A company culture that doesn't match your needs is probably one where you just won't fit in, which means it's not likely to take you very far.

■ ■ ■

No matter what the job, there are certain qualities that all top-performing employees share. These are skills applicable to almost any kind of work. They're portable. You can take them with you from job to job. Master them and you are master of your fate.

1. Time management. Making the most of your time boosts productiv- ity and efficiency. Make to-do lists. Keep your schedule up-to-date. Prioritize projects and goals. Meet deadlines.

2. Be dependable. You want to be the go-to person in your office. That doesn't mean you have to be a pushover, the guy everybody dumps work upon. It does mean that when you agree to do a job, you do the job. On time and on budget.

3. Look and act promotable. You've got a job, but unless you plan to make it the last job you ever have, think long-term. Act like you're a man or woman on a mission, always prepared to take the next step, to take your career to the next level. Dress accordingly. In fact, dress for the job you want, not the job you have. Showcase your work when you can. Go above and beyond.

4. Create value in everything you do. Don't just cross things off a to-do list. If you have a job to do, do it well. Commit your best effort to all tasks, large and small. That might be challenging at times, but people notice.

5. Be resourceful. Think outside the box. If you're doing a job and you see a better way to do it, speak up (in a polite, respectful way). Anticipate problems and find answers before they're needed. Don't be afraid to do a little legwork, a little sweating before it's necessary. It will always pay off.

6. Get noticed. There's nothing wrong with stepping up and stepping out: Volunteer for extra duties. Look for chances to be part of a team. Likewise look for chances to work with other departments, both to learn about that department but also to meet new people. And always offer to work with key customers. They are your magic carpet to being invaluable to your company. If the company's largest customer loves you, your boss will love you too. Your visibility and success will rise as others think of you when the next big, exciting project comes around.

7. Stay informed. Become an expert in your field. That includes staying on top of industry news and trends, company policies, department memos, etc. Read the company newsletter. Talk to others in the know. The more information you have at hand, the better prepared you will be when opportunity comes knocking.

8. Keep positive. No matter what's going on, remain level-headed, upbeat, with your eye on the prize. There are always ups and downs but focus on the long-term. If you have a temper, it is your—and only your— responsibility to never show it at work.

9. Be a team player. This is about more than just getting along with others or telling a good joke. In meetings or group efforts, you want to be seen as a valued contributor who offers feedback, meets deadlines, gets things done—all for the common good. Know your teammates, their strengths and strive to make them look good too.

10. Conduct effective meetings. The best way to not get anything done is to call a meeting. That's a little harsh but meetings are probably the most abused aspect of the workday. The best meetings are short, sweet and to the point. If you're calling the meeting or running it, make sure you have an agenda and stick to it. Make sure only the people that need to be at the meeting are there. Stay on point. Allow everyone to speak who wants to speak, but keep them focused on the subject. Try to complete all of the tasks of the meeting before the meeting ends. If that's not possible, assign action items with due dates.

11. Be a leader. You don't need an impressive title to be a leader. You need the requisite attributes: Initiative. Persuasiveness. A sense of responsibility. Creativity. Fearlessness. Want more details: Read John Wooden's 1997 book (with Steve Jamieson), *Wooden: A Lifetime of Observations and Reflections On and Off the Court.* One of the all-time great basketball coaches and an even-greater molder of young men, Wooden reflects upon what he learned in a lifetime of teaching about basketball and life. It's heartfelt and brilliant. (There's also a 2005 follow-up by Wooden and Jamieson called *Wooden on Leadership: How to Create a Winning Organization.*)

■ ■ ■

All forms of communication are important. You know you need to speak clearly, concisely and get to the point as quickly as possible. If you have a heavy accent that often others cannot understand, it is your obligation to speak slowly and enunciate. When in a professional environment, do your very best to speak without the accent. This is not to hide your ethnicity or background. It is your problem if people cannot understand you. In the long run you will be the loser, not them.

And then there is email. In some ways email has supplanted the phone as the most common form of business communication. However, don't use email in place of a phone call or face-to-face meeting. It is impersonal and might be counter-productive.

But when you do email for business, follow these basic rules:

- Pique the recipient's curiosity with a descriptive subject line. If it's not, there's a decent chance the recipient won't even open up the email.
- Begin with a greeting and end with a close. Include contact information.
- Watch your tone. Don't use all UPPERCASE letters, which is commonly perceived as a sort of digitized yelling. Use proper grammar and punctuation.
- Be brief. People get lots of emails. If yours are like books, people will learn not to open them.
- If you have attachments, mention them in the body of the email so that the recipient will know to look for them.
- Proofread before you transmit. A badly written email with misspellings is not the image you want to send. And watch out for spell-check. It can be your enemy. I have a terrible time spelling "inconvenient." My spell-check often changes it to "incontinent." Not exactly the meaning I intended.

Dare I Ask for a Raise?

So you're doing great. Heck, better than great. What's next? Well, that's actually the subject of the last chapter, but let's finish up here talking about asking for a raise. It's a tricky subject. Nobody likes doing it. It's hard to tell a boss that you think you're worth more than you're being paid, but frankly, there are times and situations when doing so makes absolutely perfect sense. The rule of thumb is that you should be in a job for at least one year before asking for a raise.

Before you step into the boss' office and say, "I'd like to discuss the potential of a raise," do a few things first and make a plan. It should include:

1. Gather supporting evidence. Build a case of facts. Collect any positive emails, letters or other documents extolling your work from clients, co-workers or others.

2. Review your skills, responsibilities and accomplishments. Assess them honestly. Look for weaknesses or places where your boss might question you. Figure out your answers in advance.

3. Know your market value. How much is someone in your position typically paid. Where does your current salary fit into this picture? Salary sites like www.careers.wsj.com, www.salary.com and www.jobsmart.org can help.

4. Be willing to negotiate. You want to have a figure in mind for a raise, but it might not legitimately be possible for the company to meet that expectation. Negotiate in good faith and expect the same from your boss. If your boss can't satisfy your requested raise, perhaps you can get other perks sweetened: additional vacation days or permission to work from home one day a week, for example. Go into the meeting with a list of options other than cash that mean a lot to you but don't cost the company money.

5. Be professional. Make an appointment. Don't corner your boss in the elevator or ambush him at lunch. Make a formal presentation, with all of the necessary bells and whistles. And give the boss time to consider your requests and to get back to you. He may have to get permission from his boss or just get comfortable with the changes you asked for.

And conversely, here are a few things you *should not* do:

1. Don't say you "need" a raise. No boss wants to hear about your rent increase. Do show why you deserve one.

2. Don't be afraid. If you can prove you're worth it, then you are worth it and your boss is likely to welcome the chance to reward you.

3. Don't make threats. Scare tactics don't prove anything except that maybe you're not the right person for the job. If you threaten to leave if you don't get the raise, someone may call your bluff and show you the door.

4. Don't beg. You want to appear confident in yourself and in your value to the company.

5. Don't ask for a raise just because someone else got one. Unless it is an issue for the Equal Employment Opportunity Commission, every employee should be compensated in relation to his or her own value to the company.

If you've done your homework and the timing is right, a requested raise will likely be yours. Congratulations! But if it doesn't happen or you don't get everything you asked for and there are lots of legitimate reasons why you didn't—do not be disconsolate. It's not the end of the world. Ask your boss for reasons why a raise was not possible. Ask if there is something you can do to better your chances of earning more in the future. Accept any feedback with a professional demeanor and a determination to use the knowledge to improve your value to the company.

 ## Playing Nicely with Others

It takes a lot of different types of people to create a workplace. The office environment is like any other place where people gather together: There will be natural leaders, followers, motivators, slackers, overachievers and ne'er-do-wells. Every office is different, but every office has some basic personality types. To be effective and successful, you'll need to work with all of them. That means learning what makes each type tick, and how to interact with their different styles. Here's a basic chart:

PERSONALITY	DESCRIPTION	MAY SAY	HOW TO DEAL
Pessimist	Always negative, second-guessing	"Things will never improve."	Use facts, focus on the positive
Gossip	Spreads rumors, misinformation	"Did you hear…"	Avoid conversations, be skeptical
Resister	Doesn't like change, stubborn, recalcitrant	"I liked it better the old way…"	Introduce change gradually, show value
Perfectionist	Unrealistic standards, micromanages	"It could be better still."	Set realistic goals
Know-it-all	Acts like an expert, often arrogant	"My way is the right way."	Present data that proves your point, encourage open-mindedness

continued on next page

continued from previous page

Uncommitted	Doesn't take job seriously	"I'll do that later."	Set clear goals, monitor closely
Bully	Steamrolls over everyone, lacks social skills	"Do it now."	Stand up for self
Credit grabbers	Always looking out for themselves at expense of others	"That was my idea."	Put your name on everything you do; don't let others take credit for your work

Invariably, there will be people who you will struggle to work with. Some folks are simply jerks, lazy, chronically angry, obnoxious or worse. As much as you can, identify them quickly and try to stay clear. But if you can't, do the following (even if it's hard):

- Treat them like customers
- Be genuine
- Smile
- Don't get angry yourself
- Recognize that an attitude problem exists
- Help them take responsibility
- Acknowledge the underlying cause for the negativity, if you can
- Be tough
- Be positive
- Be a good team player

Also find a way to make your mutual boss aware of the challenge you are dealing with and what you are trying to do to make the best of the situation. But if it is affecting your work, or the perception of your work, then you need to do something about it. It is probably affecting the work effectiveness of the department in ways that the boss is not even aware of. If the boss does not see it as a problem and the situation is intolerable for you, then you need to call up your Career Manager and make some things happen.

The yang to the yin of office politics is office etiquette.

 Office Etiquette

There are proper and appropriate ways to behave in any social situation, including your workplace. In fact, it's particularly important that you know how to act at work, given that it's where you will spend many of your waking hours and upon which you depend for your livelihood.

Good business etiquette basically boils down to three things: integrity, politeness and consideration. Treat everyone with respect, from the president of the company to the guy who takes the lunch orders. Be a good listener. Be on time to meetings. Offer congratulations happily. Return calls and emails in a timely fashion. Be careful with humor. Don't swear. Be considerate of others' workloads. Say "please" and "thank you." All of the things I suggested you do during the interview process to make sure you are noticed are the same things to do once you have the job...so that you get noticed. Amazing how that works!

 Office Politics

Whether you're employed at a business with just a handful of co-workers or labor within a corporation with hundreds or thousands of fellow cogs, there will always be "office politics." Office politics is different from office gossip. Office gossip may strictly be a social activity (good or bad); but office politics is pursued with the objective of gaining some sort of workplace advantage, such as a raise, a better office or just the attention of the boss.

When you're new on the job, office politics are often confusing and occasionally treacherous. Every worker occasionally engages in a little office politicking at various times. It's part of the process of getting noticed, though it should be practiced sparingly and always with integrity and respect for others. Use it to help your cause, not to knock down someone else's.

For the most part, the best way to engage in office politics is just to avoid it. Stay above the fray. Here are some tips to help:

- Choose your words carefully, but be honest and sincere
- Compliment a lot, criticize just a little

continued on next page

continued from previous page

- Avoid gossip and rumor-mongering
- Be positive
- Stay out of the line of fire—don't get involved in matters that don't involve you
- Help everyone
- Empathize with others
- Disagree without disrespect or condescension
- Learn how to connect and relate

 ## Smaller Versus Bigger

The size of a company usually dictates its organizational style.

Smaller companies are often reflections of the owner; what the boss says goes. Bigger companies tend to have a management hierarchy, a system through which decisions are made, often via committees.

Smaller companies are usually less formal than bigger companies, which likely have policies, procedures and maybe handbooks for almost every issue.

Smaller companies have fewer opportunities in traditional roles, but often provide more flexibility and opportunity to do many things, especially early in a career. This is very true in our company. Mel and I will work until we drop so there is very little opportunity for our staff to grow to the top jobs. So our challenge is to keep our good staff challenged and compensated in ways that make up for this lack of mobility at the top. But that's another book.

Larger companies usually have more positions, more departments and more chances to find new or different roles or duties.

One size doesn't fit all. Whether it's better to work for a smaller company or a bigger company depends upon individual circumstance. There are benefits to each. Only you can decide which is better for you at each stage in your career. You may want to strategically flow in and out of different sized companies and public versus privately-owned companies at different times to gain certain experience.

phil•osophy 101

The great comedian George Burns once said, "I look to the future because that's where I'm going to spend the rest of my life." Since the guy once played the role of God in the 1977 movie Oh, God!, presumably he knew what he was talking about.

Here's my point: The goal and theme of this book has been to help you find yourself, at least in the sense of helping you find yourself a career. But the work doesn't end with work. Or the last page of this book. Feel free to read it again at different stages of your career.

Once you've settled into a new place of employment, it's easy and natural to turn off the jets, close down the networks, heave a sigh of relief and just focus on the work at hand.

And to a great degree, that is exactly what you should do. The preceding chapter was all about how to establish yourself in your new job—and how to excel: Goal-setting, team-playing, and staying organized. These are just some of the things you should actively put effort into and pursue. You need to take them seriously!

On the other hand, unless you've just landed the dream job of a lifetime (defined as a job you literally would enjoy doing every day for the rest of your work life, one that you might pay to do) and your employer has given you an iron-clad contract guaranteeing permanent employment (including regular, acceptable cost-of-living adjustments, pay raises, etc.), no matter how poorly or inadequately you perform now or in the future, it's wise to think about your next job, the one you haven't yet imagined or begun pursuing.

That's because no job lasts forever. Just look around. Everybody knows the story of somebody who lost a job through no fault of his or her own. Maybe he was usurped by a younger, better co-worker. Maybe she was fired as part of a corporate cutback or restructuring. Maybe they messed up and deserved it.

If you are reading this now and say none of this applies to me, I love my job, I love my boss, I love my industry, I love my company...and they all love me and I am essential to the success of the company, they can't live without me...then consider this your wake up call. Life changes, new competitors appear every day, new technology appears every day, and the boss's daughter appears on the horizon and he thinks she is more loved than you. Have your radar on at all times, watching your company, your competitors, management changes in your company and any other extraneous changes that might affect your job. Don't ever be complacent and assume conditions that affect your career will never change. Instead be proactive.

For our purposes, the particular reason doesn't matter. If you're out of work now because you were fired, laid off or quit isn't the point. The point is that you're out of work. Or you were out of work. Or you woke up and hated your job and you did something about it. Now you've got a job that you really enjoy. Cherish it, but also start thinking about what happens next in your working world. Always be preparing for anything to happen.

Phil

Managing
your career

9

> **"When it comes to the future, there are three kinds of people:
> those who let it happen, those who make it happen, and those
> who wonder what happened."**
> — JOHN M. RICHARDSON

> **"The future is always beginning now."**
> — MARK STRAND

> **"The best way to predict the future is to invent it."**
> — ALAN KAY

Stuff happens. Things change. We just don't always notice it until—BOOM!
I like to compare this notion to the tectonic plates that are shifting beneath
our feet. They move small distances each year until so much pressure builds
up that CRACK! RUMBLE! POW!, we have a huge earthquake that no one
saw coming or could have forecast.

Let's discuss two basic ways of thinking about this.

The first is the most obvious: You have developed a long-term career
plan that involves a series of jobs that serve as stepping stones to an
ultimate aspiration. That's good. Everyone should have a plan. It should be
flexible enough to accommodate new factors or unforeseen change. Either
that or you're willing to regularly revisit the plan and amend it as needed.

If you don't yet have a career plan in hand, do it now. Unlike some of
the other lists I've asked you to create, this list is about goals, short- and
long-term, stuff you haven't done yet. Short-term goals are generally those
that can be achieved within a few months or a year. They're often stepping
stones to longer-term goals, which may take three to five years to achieve.

Your career plan describes the steps you'll take to reach your goals.
Usually the goal is a particular career objective: You want to be president

of a company, own your own business, earn a certain income. Here are some questions to ask yourself as you shape your career plan:

- What do I love to do?
- What do I want to do?
- What motivates me?
- How far do I want to go?
- How will I get there?
- Who will help me?
- Am I willing to make any sacrifices? What kind?
- What do I do next?

Your career plan is a roadmap, but there is no single way to get to your objective. Your plan can be a basic checklist, a time schedule or a 100-page, detailed document, complete with footnotes and annotations. Whatever works for you.

If you're stuck on how to start, start simple. Make a list with four headings:

CAREER PLAN

POSITION	TIMELINE	STEPS TO TAKE	RESOURCES NEEDED
Bank Teller	June 2012	Finance BA	Scholarships
Vault Manager	July 2013	Certification	Education Reimbursement
Loan Manager	September 2014	CRE Credentials	Savings Reimbursement
Branch Manager	January 2016	MBA	
Regional Manager	January 2020	Pacific School of Banking	
Area Manager	January 2025		

Once you've filled it out, don't file it away somewhere to be forgotten. This is a living document. You should review it at least twice a year to evaluate where you are and make necessary revisions.

The second mode involves maintaining an internal conversation with yourself about what you're doing for a living now. Are you following your Career Plan? Are you meeting your timeline? How's work going? Are you satisfied? Are there things you'd like to do, or do differently? Is it in your power to make changes? Are there changes that need to be made?

On the flip side, how are you perceived by your boss, upper management and your co-workers? Do they think you're doing a great job? Are you exceeding their expectations or just meeting them? The latter happens more often than you might think. I've met and helped many people who firmly believed they brought something unique and invaluable to their jobs, that they were so highly prized and admired by their companies and colleagues that nothing untoward would ever happen to *them*.

Then they got laid off.

Know When to Go

One key to knowing when it's time to begin looking for a new job is an honest evaluation of your current employer's condition. What are your company's vital signs? Is it healthy and thriving, with a good revenue stream, steady expansion and reinvestment in new technology and research? Or is it struggling, overextended, on the verge of bankruptcy or closure? In your industry, are larger companies circling, ready to swoop down and buy companies like the one where you are now working? If not, will they be soon? Is that a good thing for your career or a bad thing?

These questions may or may not be easy to answer. The workers in the last buggy whip factory probably knew their days were numbered. Heck, they probably drove to their last day at work in horseless carriages.

Companies in trouble don't often broadcast their struggles if they can avoid it. Bad news generally begets more bad news. Customers shun businesses they fear won't be around tomorrow. Employees flee companies in trouble or turmoil. Nobody wants a co-worker beating them to a scarce job opportunity. Nobody wants to be the last guy to turn off the lights.

After an honest evaluation, if things are good, then stay right where you are. If things are bad, as in you are a duplication that will not survive, then red lights should be flashing and your radar should be in second gear.

Marlene is the owner of a successful, avant-garde advertising agency in San Diego. She's a bright, smart woman who held a number of different, unrelated jobs at huge companies before breaking off and building her current agency. One of those previous jobs was as vice president of public relations for what seemed to be a successful manufacturer of personal computers. Unbeknownst to her, the company's owner was in financial trouble and the company itself on the verge of insolvency. The owner needed to cut back deeply, a last-ditch effort to save the company. He asked my friend, as VP of PR, to do the nasty work of informing virtually all of the staff that they were being let go. The bad news would come down on a Friday, one worker after another.

As you can imagine, it was a horrendous day for my friend, a task she had no choice but to do. And she did. The last, laid-off employee left around 4:00 p.m. The company owner, who in a dazzling display of cowardice, had avoided any appearance during the day, showed up. He called my friend into the office and informed her that she too was being let go, though he thoughtfully thanked her and congratulated her for the great job she had done that day.

In retrospect, Marlene says there were signs of doom and disaster, though she didn't recognize them (or chose not to recognize them) at the time. In his book *Get Hired Fast! Tap the Hidden Job Market in 15 Days*, Brian Graham describes 15 situations that might be signs your career security is at risk. Keep them in mind and keep your eyes open:

1. Did the person who hired you leave? (There goes your patron.)
2. Are other key players leaving? (What do they know that you don't?)
3. Is a change of ownership in the offing? (New owners, new rules, new employees.)
4. Is there a change in reporting structure? (Bad news?)
5. Is the company's stock moving downward? (Death spiral?)
6. How is your industry doing as a whole? (Does anybody make typewriters anymore? No.)
7. How is your division or department doing? (Are you expendable?)
8. How are your major clients faring? (Sometimes you get dragged down by others.)
9. Are managers often locked away in secret meetings? (Clueless employees are happy employees.)
10. Is there a "black hole" when it comes to new contracts or projects? (Black holes are never a good sign.)
11. Do you see evidence of cash flow problems? (Where's the bleeding? Where's the fix?)
12. Are you being excluded from meetings you used to attend? (Never good news.)
13. Are your requests for help being denied? (It might be a lack of resources. It might be a lack of interest in helping you.)
14. Are you sensing strange vibes? (You'll know them when you feel them.)
15. Are you being asked to prepare for outsourcing?

There's a flip side to this coin. There are signs, too, that tell you when to move on, even if your employers love you. Graham suggests asking yourself these two questions, particularly if you're aware of opportunities elsewhere.

1. Am I getting stale (or bored) in the job? Have I peaked in terms of company advancement?
2. Is my current job an unpleasant place to be? Has something changed for the worse?

The New, Improved You

Each day on the job, you have an opportunity to get better at what you do, to learn something new and then apply it to your work. It's called experience. Unless you're asleep at the wheel, you naturally exploit past experience and build on it to get ahead.

But that's not enough now days. You need to constantly reinvent yourself into a shinier, newer model. You need to actively seek out new knowledge and learning. One of the smartest things you can do is pursue any opportunities available through your current company for training or professional education. An employer-paid education allowance is a terrible thing to waste.

This can be done formally, in the sense of seeking an advanced educational degree. If you have a bachelor's degree, consider getting a master's. If you don't have any degree, get one now. Having a spoonful of alphabet soup after your name is no guarantee of full-time employment—there are plenty of PhDs out of work—but education never hurts and almost always helps improve your marketability and attractiveness as a job candidate.

Dave found himself caught in a sticky wicket. He lived in the Los Angeles area and survived several mergers in his industry until the last one. (Isn't that always the case?) He became redundant after the latest merger, but his skills were still good and he found a similar job in Phoenix. He and his wife had young children whom they did not want to move in the middle of the school year. So Dave moved alone to Phoenix and commuted home every weekend. He and his wife's ultimate goal, however, was to live and work in San Diego, his wife's hometown.

Now, as the plot thickens, the school year ended and Dave's bosses assumed Dave would be moving his family to Phoenix—a reasonable expectation from a committed management employee, right? But Dave is not a committed employee. He is bored with the new job and wants to live in San Diego.

Issue one: How does he seek employment in San Diego when he doesn't live there, knowing he is competent in his industry with equally qualified job seekers who already live there. By the way, we employers like hiring people in our communities, rather than moving them here. Doing so is more complicated and expensive. Locals almost always have an advantage over out-of-towners.

Issue two: How does Dave answer questions from his boss about the Phoenix house hunt?

Issue three: How does Dave make good use of all his free time while he is sitting in an apartment in Phoenix all week?

What would you tell Dave? The condensed version of our chat was that he should spend every free moment in San Diego network-ing and using family connections, which is how he met me. Yes, the school year is out, but they have not been able to sell their house and can't move until it sells. Also, use his time to start working on an MBA degree. It will help him in any career, but it will especially impress any interviewer.

Also consider certification programs. If your chosen field of work is one in which skills can be advanced and recognized through formalized training programs, by all means pursue them. Again, they don't guarantee a pay raise or a better job, but they almost always help and set you apart from others who haven't shown similar initiative.

Finally, there are informal and indirect ways to improve your employ-ability, such as staying on top of the latest computer skills or learning a second language. If your employer doesn't offer such programs, look into taking classes at the local community college, extension course programs, professional groups or industry associations. Other options are online programs, personal tutors and self-help books.

How do you know what kind of class to take or language to learn? That's easy. Stay informed. Read everything: newspapers, magazines, websites, blogs, trade journals. Soak up information like a sponge. You never know what tidbit you learn today will be useful tomorrow.

In terms of your specific career, ask your boss.

"Mr. Jones, I really enjoy working here at Acme Industries. I certainly enjoy the accounting department. Where else could you see me being able to utilize my talents and grow within the company, and add more value? Hmmm... interesting. What skills and education would I need to succeed in that department?"

Serious kiss-up? You bet! Was the boss wowed? Probably. May be the first time an employee has ever talked to him that way. Did you get some great insight into what your boss thinks about the job you are doing and your future with Acme? You may not like what he had to say and now it is your time to react. You obviously did not talk about any options outside of Acme, but depending on what the boss said, it may be time to rev up a new job search. This search will be at your leisure while you have a job, rather than after being surprised and let go.

It's always smart to know what's happening not just in your company and your industry, but also in other industries. This will let you anticipate what your boss or company will be looking for in their next hire. One way to do this is to peruse job boards and postings on a regular basis. Even if you're not actually looking for a job, it's beneficial to see what employers want. Ask yourself a couple of questions as you scan the listings: Are there any commonalities among the jobs being offered? Do they seem to all want qualities like good communication skills, presentation experience or expertise with a particular kind of software, tool or technique? If they do, and you don't think your abilities or experience quite fit or meet the need, maybe these are areas you should pursue in terms of additional training or education.

Keep the Net Open

As I have said throughout this book, it's important to keep your network open and operating. It's like building a house. You labor mightily to lay the foundation, put up the walls and roof, paint and furnish it. Once you move into the house, it's all about maintenance, keeping your new home in good shape.

Your network of business-related contacts, sources, colleagues and friends are no different. You must nurture this network because it is the foundation upon which your career rests. The job you have—or the job you will have next—is quite likely not the last job of your life. You'll need your network again.

So "circle back," take the time and effort every few months or so to email or phone members of your network. Arrange to get together for lunch or catch up on the news. Update phone numbers and addresses. It's important to create an efficient, simple, easy way of keeping track of your network. You can do that any number of ways, but the relevant information you want to keep in mind and at hand are:

- Name
- Title
- Employer
- Hobbies
- Industry
- Professional associations
- How you know this person
- Where you met

And anything else that might be of interest in the future. You might also note when you last spoke or met, what you talked about, if you asked anything of them or they of you.

That may sound like a lot of work—and maybe it is—but keeping your network viable and up-to-date is a lot less laborious than reviving or starting a network when you need to look for a new job.

And besides, these people are supposed to be important to you, so why wouldn't you want to stay up-to-date with them? Which brings up a related point: Don't call the people in your network only when you need a favor or assistance. You want people to know you value them for themselves, that you're interested not only in whom they're LinkedIn with, but who they are. Birthdays are always a good way to stay in touch.

Conversely, members of your network should know you're there for them as well if they need a hand. Be proactive about it. If you can help, help. Indeed, look for opportunities to be of assistance, even if it takes some effort on your part. Good deeds pay off, in all ways. Pay a good deed forward.

When Do I Use My Network?

You've worked hard to keep your network of friends and colleagues up and running like a finely tuned racecar. That's great. The question is, when do you actually hop into the car and drive it? Odds are, you'll know the answer when you need it, but here are some times when you might want to tap into your network:

- You're thinking about a new career
- You're investigating a particular career field
- You're working through a professional challenge or crisis
- You're requesting references or referrals
- You're spreading word that you're seeking new career opportunities
- You're looking for a new job

And That's the Way it Is

I always tell my audiences that if I ever make a job search or long-term career planning seem easy, they have the right to call me out on it. The process is not easy, never will be, and if it ever is then we have a host of new problems. We will be living under the cloud of very slow job growth for many years to come. That's the reality of our "new economy." But thousands of people are getting new jobs in our country, and in your community, every day: Why shouldn't you be one of them? Why shouldn't you be among the 10% who love their jobs or at least the next 40% who really like their jobs? There is no reason. If you are willing to put the work into managing your job search and continually managing your career, I guarantee you that you will be among those of us looking forward to going to work every day.

But it does take work. I hope you have found value in reading *Job Won!*, maybe even enjoyed it. Life is too short to take ourselves too seriously—I hope we never lose our sense of humor, including being able to laugh at ourselves. But when it's time to get serious and plan a goal for ourselves, we have to have a map to get there. We also must be empowered to get out of our comfort zone. For most of us, searching for a new job is definitely out of that comfort zone. I have found, though, that once I am confident that I know what I am doing, why I am doing it, and have the tools to do what I need to do, my comfort zone really expands. I hope yours does, too. And I hope *Job Won!* empowers you.

There are really two themes in this book: one is how to manage a job search when you are out of work and the other is how to manage your long-term career to make sure it is fulfilling, by your standards, and not anyone else's. Now I want you to look back through the book and see if there is anything I suggested you do that you are not capable of doing. I doubt there is. Probably the most common pushback I get is people saying they are uncomfortable approaching strangers for help. They are not comfortable networking. We have a very simple exercise in our Strategies for Success training program that you should try. Attendees are asked to strike up a conversation with a complete stranger every day for two weeks. The perfect example is standing in line at the grocery store. There are people in front of you and behind you. They, too, are bored. There racks of candies and magazines right in front of you. How easy is it to ask the person next to you which candy is their favorite? At first our students find it awkward, but by the end of the class, they are regular extroverts.

But life takes us on some twists and turns that we never expected. We need to approach these twists as interesting opportunities and not fight them. Once they know strangers would not hesitate to approach them, it all seems alright. And trust me, you get used to it. Remember I was a shy kid, and, boy, did I get over that!

I am convinced networking will have the biggest influence in your future job searches, planned or unplanned, for many years. Why? Because as my fellow HR professionals use more and more automation and technology in conducting candidate searches, we will fall back even more on who we personally know and who comes personally recommended to us. It's almost like we are running away from too much technology in the HR world and reaching out for real people. And real people come recommended to us because of all our new friends, like you, that we meet networking. Some people say that up to 80% of new jobs are found because of some level of networking.

What makes the job search and career management doable is the "Career Manager" I talked about. You! It sometimes feels like Sybil, the lady with multiple personalities. Sometimes you are the client and sometimes you are the counselor. Just like sometimes you are the pigeon and sometimes you are the statue! Remember, as you are watching out for yourself, you are inherently watching out for your family, too. That thought alone is very motivating.

Remember David from Chapter 2? He fell into his banking career because of a summer job. He had to earn money for college. He liked

banking, was good at it and it was comfortable. David graduated, the bank offered him a job, he didn't have to search the want ads (yes, back then they were "want ads"), he didn't have to interview and said "why not?", maybe even adding "until something better comes along." I call this the career coast. You turn around 20 years later and you are still working in the field that you like, but are not passionate about, treading water until some wakeup call comes. In David's case we know it was a layoff. Other reasons could be a meltdown, either on purpose or subconsciously, where you get yourself fired or made irrelevant. Watch out for all these reasons; they are not good ones career wise.

Let's look at what David did do when the wakeup call came. He fantasized about his ideal job. When he dissected his ideal job, what were the components that excited him? Where could those components of the ideal job be found in reality? He made a list, researched each one, narrowed his options down with a dose of practicality and networked like crazy in his new chosen field. In David's case, his ever present radar led him to hearing about someone else changing jobs and thereby opening up a position that fit his criteria.

David methodically listed the strengths he would bring to the job, understood his weaknesses, and how to overcome them, networked some more, practiced his interview skills and Eureka—got the job!

David is still at that job. In fact he is considering whether he has another career in him before he retires for good. David tells me he is enjoying, for the first time, the satisfaction of not coasting into a career. Instead, by being proactive in his career choice, he is learning new skills and dealing with new challenges. Now he is afraid he is addicted to this new excitement and is questioning whether he wants to start the entire process all over again in a new career path.

My suggestion to David was that if he is still enjoying his current position there is no need to make a cut-and-run decision yet. Ramp up the job radar again and pay attention to what comes your way. If something of interest hits you over the head or bubbles up during cocktail hour, then there is plenty of time to investigate the opportunity. Find something you fall in love with and it's decision time. Until then, enjoy your current position and as Scarlett O'Hara said, "I'll worry about that tomorrow."

If you are searching for a job or a career or currently working and want to make sure you are not on a dead end path, then listen to your Career Manager, heed the advice, know it will be good for you and then make it happen. I have complete faith in you and just wish that I could be there to hear all of your success stories, and help you celebrate when you hear "You're Hired!"

Now, Coach, go forth and make it happen!

 ## Somebody's Got to Do It

In our lives, we will all have many jobs—and likely many careers. The days of a gold watch after 50 years with the same employers are over, assuming they ever really existed. I mean, really, have you ever met anybody who worked for the same company for generations and has a timepiece to prove it?

My point is this: You'll probably do a lot of things to earn a living, and some are likely to have little to do with your interests or long-term aspirations. Before you become rich and famous, you might have to follow in the footsteps of these celebrities and their one-time occupations:

- Jim Carrey, security guard
- Sean Connery, milkman
- Simon Cowell, mail room clerk
- Michael Dell (the computer guy), dishwasher
- Danny DeVito, hairdresser
- Walt Disney, paperboy
- Harrison Ford, carpenter
- Hugh Jackman, clown
- Mick Jagger, ice cream salesman
- Madonna, doughnut shop worker
- Demi Moore, debt collection agent
- Brad Pitt, refrigerator mover
- Sylvester Stallone, lion cage cleaner
- Rod Stewart, gravedigger
- Barbara Walters, secretary